CW01018173

IDEOLOGY AND SOCIAL SCIENCE

André Béteille is Professor Emeritus of Sociology in the University of Delhi. He has held visiting appointments at Cambridge, the London School of Economics, Erasmus University, Rotterdam, and various other institutions in Europe and America. He was also a Fellow at the Institute for Advanced Study, Berlin, and a Visiting Fellow at the Institute for Advanced Study in the Humanities, Edinburgh. He was a Jawaharlal Nehru Fellow from 1968 to 1970, and received the Jawaharlal Nehru National Award of the Government of Madhya Pradesh in 1994.

Apart from his newspaper articles, he has published extensively in scholarly periodicals in India and abroad. His books include *Caste, Class and Power, Studies in Agrarian Social Structure*, and *Society and Politics in India*. The book of readings entitled *Social Inequality*, edited by him and published by Penguin Books in 1969, has been used in the teaching of sociology worldwide. A previous collection of newspaper articles was published by Penguin Books India in 2000 under the title *Chronicles of Our Time*.

Professor Béteille is a Corresponding Fellow of the British Academy and an Honorary Fellow of the Royal Anthropological Institute.

By the same author:

Chronicles of Our Time

Ideology and Social Science

ANDRÉ BÉTEILLE

Foreword by Ramachandra Guha

PENGUIN BOOKS

PENGUIN BOOKS
Published by the Penguin Group
Penguin Books India Pvt Ltd, 11 Community Centre, Panchsheel Park, New
Delhi 110 017, India
Penguin Group (USA) Inc., 375 Hudson Street, New York, New York 10014,
USA
Penguin Group (Canada), 90 Eglinton Avenue East, Suite 700, Toronto,
M4P 2Y3 (a division of Pearson Penguin Canada Inc.)
Penguin Books Ltd, 80 Strand, London WC2R 0RL, England
Penguin Ireland, 25 St Stephen's Green, Dublin 2, Ireland (a division of
Penguin Books Ltd)
Penguin Group (Australia), 250 Camberwell Road, Camberwell, Victoria
3124, Australia (a division of Pearson Australia Group Pty Ltd)
Penguin Group (NZ), cnr Airborne and Rosedale Roads, Albany, Auckland
1310, New Zealand (a division of Pearson New Zealand Ltd)
Penguin Group (South Africa) (Pty) Ltd, 24 Sturdee Avenue, Rosebank,
Johannesburg 2196, South Africa

Penguin Books Ltd, Registered Offices: 80 Strand, London WC2R 0RL,
England

First published by Penguin Books India 2006

Copyright © André Béteille 2006

10 9 8 7 6 5 4 3 2 1

ISBN-13: 978-0-14306-201-1   ISBN-10: 0-14306-201-8

Typeset in Sabon by Mantra Virtual Services, New Delhi
Printed at Baba Barkhanath Printers, New Delhi

For Mr Shyam Lal
Journalist and Bibliophile
with appreciation and gratitude

Contents

III

Village, Caste and Family

IV

The Indian Identity

V

Inequality and Class

VI

Discrimination and Reservation

VII

State and Civil Society

Acknowledgements

The articles put together here were first published in the editorial pages of various newspapers. The date and place of publication are indicated in each case except one which is being published here for the first time. I am grateful to the editors of the newspapers for offering me the hospitality of their columns. As I said in an earlier collection published by Penguin Books India, *Chronicles of Our Time*, I am an academic and not a journalist. Putting my ideas together within the compass of a newspaper article has always been a struggle. I am happy to say that this struggle continues and that I have no intention for the present of giving it up.

I would like to thank Rudrangshu Mukherjee of *The Telegraph* and Malini Parthasarathi of *The Hindu* for the interest they have shown in my writing, and for their unfailing courtesy. I would also like to thank Ramachandra Guha for finding the time to write the Foreword. Let me be the first to acknowledge that his praise of me is extravagant, and that it speaks more for his generosity than my desert.

André Béteille

Foreword:
The Wisest Man (Still) in India

Ramachandra Guha

Some years ago, in an assessment of André Béteille's scholarly career, I concluded that 'it can safely be said that only one other Indian, Amartya Sen, has written so consistently and so consistently well on questions of importance to his discipline and his society'. That was an *academic* judgement, based on the quality and depth of the work of these two scholars, this in contrast to 'the publication lists of the most highly regarded of this country's social scientists [which] are embarrassingly thin'.* But the more I think of it, the more the juxtaposition makes sense, and not just in terms of formal scholarship. It is also personal biography and cultural history that compel a joint consideration of the life and work of Amartya Sen and André Béteille.

Consider, first, the facts that they were of the same age, from the same province, and citizens of the same country. Sen was born in 1933; Béteille a year later. Both grew up in Bengal, speaking Bengali; both stayed on in the western side of the

---

* 'The Career and Credo of André Béteille', in Ramachandra Guha and Jonathan Parry, editors, *Institutions and Inequalities: Essays in Honour of André Béteille* (New Delhi: Oxford University Press, 1999), p. 20.

province after partition and independence. They were old enough to have had some experience of the national movement, and also of the horrors of the last decade of the Raj—of the Bengal famine and Hindu–Muslim violence in particular. And they came of age in the 1950s, thus to partake of the enthusiasm and idealism of that first decade in the history of this nation.

Sen became a professional economist; Béteille, a professional sociologist. Neither was bound by the conventions and limitations of his chosen discipline. Sen's economics was shaped by his interest in philosophy, and to a lesser extent in history and sociology. Béteille too was a genuine inter-disciplinarian: a sociologist in continuous conversation with his colleagues in anthropology, economics, and the law. This departure from narrow specialism might, in each case, have had something to with the fact that they were Bengali; reared in an intellectual climate that privileged multi-facetedness, and over which towered the shadow of that myriad-minded man, Rabindranath Tagore.

Sen and Béteille were wide-ranging in their intellectual interests, and also in the genres they wrote in. Their international reputation is based in good measure on theoretical papers published in learned journals. But both wrote extensively on questions of public policy, particularly (but not exclusively) with reference to India. And both also wrote in newspapers and mass-circulation magazines, seeking out Indians other than their own students and colleagues. Whether addressing the scholar or the layman, both also wrote with a lucidity of style still unusual in Indians who take to English, and altogether exceptional in a jargon-ridden academia.

Both Sen and Béteille were thoroughbred professionals. In fact, they were more. Their profession became their *calling*. (This steadfast devotion, over decades, to the craft of independent and original research helps explain why, in comparison to their colleagues, they wrote so well and so much.) Both sought to keep scholarship separate from political currents; in the terms of the title of this book collection, both made a clear separation between 'ideology' and 'social science'. Yet both saw that the questions they dealt with in their research were of compelling interest and importance to their society. And so they came also to write for a wider audience than that constituted by their peers.

Neither Sen nor Béteille were ever ideologists. Neither identified with a particular political party. Yet, there was a profound moral centre to their work. Both were known for their academic contributions to the study of social inequality; both were also known for their strong commitment to liberalism and constitutional democracy. These preferences and choices were not accidental. Rather, they were intimately linked to the circumstances of their upbringing. A sensitive, intelligent, young scholar living through the Bengal of the 1940s would tend, in later life, to promote the values of cultural pluralism and social justice. It helped that there were greater men who had trodden that path—in particular, Rabindranath Tagore, Mohandas K. Gandhi, and Jawaharlal Nehru. As much as purely scholarly influences, the example of this trinity lay behind the work of Sen and Béteille. They were never party men, but they were always *patriots*, upholding the idea of India forged by the likes of Tagore, Gandhi and Nehru.

There was, then, much that brought Amartya Sen and André Béteille together, much that permits us to see them as standing alongside and with one another. Yet it would be incorrect to altogether ignore the things that drew them apart. Their careers were somewhat similar and comparable, yet also different and, in the end, *individual*. Although in a cultural sense a Bengali, Béteille's father was French. Sen was more authentically *bhadralok*: in fact, his lineage was as impeccable as it could possibly be. His adored grandfather was a highly respected professor in Santiniketan, and the name 'Amartya' was chosen by Tagore himself. Béteille was brought up middle class; he studied at St Xavier's College and Calcutta University.

Sen was born into the intellectual aristocracy; he studied at Presidency College and the University of Cambridge. Béteille spent four decades teaching at a single place: the Sociology Department of the Delhi School of Economics. Sen's first job was at Jadavpur University; he also taught for eight years at the Delhi School of Economics. But most of his professional life was spent overseas, as a professor at Oxford, Cambridge, the London School of Economics, and Harvard.

This last fact was not irrelevant to a difference in intellectual orientation that was slight, but by no means insignificant. Both Sen and Béteille were conspicuously broad-minded, intellectually as well as culturally. Both were simultaneously Indian and of the world. However, while Béteille stayed in India and never lost sight of the wider world, Sen lived overseas yet never lost touch with his native land. In their work, read closely, were revealed subtle differences of emphasis. In Béteille's writing were many references to specific Indian debates and controversies—to a particular law changed or enacted, a particular intervention by a scholar or politician. Sen's allusions were usually broader, to various competing ideas of India. This was probably related to the fact that, while his commitment to his country could never be gainsaid, Sen lived mostly apart from the heat and the action.

Even if Sen had lived in India, or Béteille in Cambridge, there would yet have been divergences in their intellectual approach and scholarly production. For one, while economics is more prone to abstraction and generalization, sociology is more empirical. True, Sen was an economist with a keen interest in the 'field-view', while Béteille was perhaps the only Indian sociologist with a serious interest in theory. And both, as I have noted, were never disciplinary chauvinists. Still, the fact remains that they practised different disciplines, with different traditions, research agendas, and methods of presentation, these all reflected in the books and essays published under their names.

But there were also (and again, admittedly subtle) differences that go beyond the disciplines. Sen's world-view was deeply shaped by the example of Tagore and, to a lesser extent, of Gandhi. Béteille admired Tagore, and respected Gandhi, but in many ways he was influenced most by the third, now much unfairly demonized member of this trinity, Jawaharlal Nehru. (This identification also explains why Béteille was so interested in the fate and future of policies and laws enacted during Nehru's long tenure as India's first prime minister.) Again, while both Sen and Béteille were liberals who had many encounters with socialism in general and Marxism in particular, Sen's came principally through personal contact (with leftist friends in Calcutta and Cambridge), whereas Béteille's had more to do with intellectual engagement, as manifest in his many essays on the close but also contentious relationship between Marxism and sociology.

One must note and acknowledge what brought Béteille and Sen together, yet one must also be grateful for what set them apart. That one was a sociologist, the other an economist; that one lived chiefly in India, the other mostly in the West; that one was a liberal and the other a fellow travelling liberal; that one admired Nehru more but the other Tagore—these (and other) differences ultimately gave rise to two different yet equally impressive bodies of work. We can read Béteille, and we can read Sen—and learn from them both.

If I have so far spoken of Béteille and Sen in the past tense, it is because their careers are now five decades old, old enough for a younger scholar to take the 'long view'. But of course they are happily very productive still, active in shaping scholarly enquiry and in communicating with a wide and, one must hope, grateful public. As I write, André Béteille serves as chairman of the Indian Council of Social Science Research, while Amartya Sen has returned to teach at Harvard on completion of his term as Master of Trinity College, Cambridge. Neither is yet done with contributing to his chosen discipline; nor, indeed, with illuminating the life and troubles of his nation. Sen has recently given us *The Argumentative Indian*; and now, in your hands, is Béteille's equally compelling collection of essays on Indian ideas, themes and debates.

II

The fifty articles in *Ideology and Social Science* cover a very wide range of subjects: from the practice of sociology to the prospects for political liberalism, from contemporary debates about caste and caste quotas to old and still persisting myths about what is said to constitute the essence of Indian culture. Each essay stands on its own. Each is carefully crafted, each rich in example and insight. Still, running through this collection are the signatures of an intellectual style that I have come to consider as being characteristic of André Béteille.

First, the sociology on offer here is consciously comparative. A fact or controversy is never analysed solely in and for itself, but with reference to other, *comparable* facts or controversies, whether occurring in the past, or in other parts of India, or other parts of the world.

Second, the sociology is comparative with regard not just to *interests* but also *ideas*. The process of secularization in India might be compared or contrasted to similar processes in France or North America. So might the practices and beliefs of scholars and ideologues. This collection bears testimony to Béteille's deep engagement with the history and intellectual traditions of lands other than his own—not just the United States and the United Kingdom (the two countries, and cultures, otherwise most familiar to Indian academics), but also Germany and Russia.

Third, there is a close attention to the complexity of social life. Ideologues tend to see things in monochromatic colours, but sociologists cannot afford to be so simple-minded. Here, Béteille is a master of his craft. He is always conscious of ambiguity and contradiction, always complicating or undermining black-and-white portraits of traditions and trends. Some Hindus like to present their religion as uniquely plural; but, as Béteille points out, this plurality of faiths and beliefs coexisted with a unique illiberalism of social practice. Some Marxists like to present themselves as always on the side of the oppressed and exploited; but, as Béteille points out, they tend to exempt from their scrutiny the manifest inequalities of the professedly 'socialist' countries. Again, he suggestively explores the disjunction between the rhetoric and practice of policies designed to promote egalitarianism, showing how some attempts at redressing inequalities have merely created new hierarchies of their own.

Fourth, in keeping with this attention to social complexity is a judiciously balanced writing style. Béteille's prose is always measured, sometimes firm, very occasionally sharp, never polemical. In his thought, as in his presentation, he abhors an excess of zeal.

Fifth, these essays show how successfully, and honourably, Béteille has stayed clear both of passing intellectual trends as well as partisan politics. He studies what he deems to be important, rather than what is deemed 'fashionable' in the global academy. He is not a member of a political party or tendency, or of a social movement or sect either. He is genuinely *independent*, in a way few Indian intellectuals are any more. The conclusions he reaches are his own. They are based on a careful examination of the evidence, not on a search for facts that fit some preconceived theory. This independence of thought and judgement means that while some of the essays reproduced here will anger the ideologues of the Hindutva movement, yet others shall gravely displease the consensual herd of the politically correct.

The title of this collection makes clear that in André Béteille's view, ideologues do not make very good social scientists. In his theoretical work, it is indeed hard to find traces of current political debates. However, in these more topical essays one can see the scholar staking out and defending a political position, which I like to think of as a distinctively *Indian* liberalism. Like Nehru and Ambedkar, and other framers of the Indian constitution, Béteille believes in the creation of a plural, free, and less unequal society, albeit by incremental and democratic means. His dislike of zeal implies a distrust of the extremes of Left and Right, of political philosophies which seek to impose their will regardless of the popular will or of future consequence. André Béteille is a self-confessed 'anti-utopian', who eschews total and complete solutions, knowing that the best is so often the enemy of the good.

III

I began with one comparison, and will now end with another. (This, I think, is in keeping with the spirit of this volume, whose author likes to say that sociology is comparative or it is not sociology at all.) This second comparison is prompted by a remark made by a colonial official nearly sixty years ago. It was in 1945 or 1946 that the outgoing Governor of Bengal, a bluff Australian named R.G. Casey, described C. Rajagopalachari as the 'wisest man in India'.

The judgement was political rather than intellectual. 'Rajaji' was a learned man, a scholar and a writer, but in praising him so, Casey was really focusing on his contributions to political dialogue and debate. In the early years of the War that had just ended, it was Rajaji who had (vainly) urged the Congress to seek a compromise with the Muslim League; and it was he who had told Gandhi that collaboration with the British would augur better for an eventual transfer of power than the oppositional 'Quit India' movement. Rajaji's advice on both counts was rejected by the Congress leadership, but its wisdom was resoundingly confirmed by later events—

this too late, however, for partition to be avoided. (A decade later, Rajaji once more proved to be wise before the event—when he urged the dismantling of what he memorably termed 'the licence-permit-quota-raj'.)

In many respects, André Béteille is the C. Rajagopalachari of our times. There are some intriguing parallels in their characters and their careers. Both only studied in India and always lived in India, yet both had a profound knowledge of English literature and Western political thought. Late in his political life, Rajaji served an incident-filled term as the first Indian governor of Bengal. Early in his life as an intellectual, Béteille spent a formative year doing fieldwork in Rajaji's native Tamil Nadu. Like Béteille, Rajaji too was deeply committed to cultural pluralism (he did more to promote Hindu–Muslim harmony and attack caste prejudice than almost any other disciple of Gandhi), and to the procedures and norms of liberal democracy. Finally, and perhaps most significantly, like Rajaji, Béteille's words of caution are seldom heard by his peers, yet often vindicated by events.

I cannot say what André Béteille will think of my comparing him with Amartya Sen, but I have no doubt that he will respond to this fresh juxtaposition with an uncharacteristic expression of zeal. He will protest that I am dishonouring the memory of a great patriot and freedom fighter, this great *builder* of modern India, by placing the name of a mere university professor alongside his. To lessen his embarrassment, let me point out that we live now in altogether less worthy times. For, when praising Rajaji as he did, R.G. Casey was sensible of the competition—this provided by Nehru, Gandhi, Patel, Ambedkar, Radhakrishnan, Azad, and many, many others.

The competition now is much diminished. That said, André Béteille remains a very wise man indeed. The wisdom is on display right through this book, which distils a lifetime of learning and reflection on matters of crucial import to India and Indians. Consider these aperçus, which are elaborated, explained, and defended in the essays that follow:

> In a constitutional democracy rights are a serious matter. They cannot be created simply in order to give expression to good intentions. The creation of rights that remain unenforced and are perhaps unenforceable damages the fabric of democracy. If we adopt the right to development as a human right who will be the bearer of the right: individuals, classes, communities or nations? How will the right be enforced? What is the kind of court in which one can seek redress when the right to development has been violated? Perhaps all that one will be able to do in the event of default will be to appeal to the conscience of the world. But in that case will it have been worthwhile to have wilfully set at naught the very wise distinction made in the Indian constitution between matters of right and matters of policy?

> It is a great mistake to believe that a hierarchical society can reconstitute itself on the basis of equality within a generation or two in a smooth and painless manner, without conflict, without violence.

> The distinctive feature of modernity, as I understand it, is that it examines the world with an open and sceptical mind. . . . No society can escape from its past, but a society should not remain tied inexorably to its past. No doubt, traditionalists believe that society can and should be improved. But they also believe that the ingredients for that improvement are to be found mainly, if not wholly, in their own social and cultural tradition. Tradition for them is a vast and inexhaustible storehouse having hidden, even unknown, treasures. . . . [On the other hand] the modernist is outward rather

than backward looking. His primary engagement is with the contemporary world which includes not just his own society but other societies as well. His engagement with his own society is with its living traditions, good as well as bad, but not necessarily with everything that lies hidden and buried in the past.

Modernization is today inescapable, but it is not a painless process, and it penalizes latecomers severely. Modernity does not presuppose a homogeneous world in which everybody does the same thing, thinks the same thoughts and speaks the same language; on the contrary, it requires and encourages knowledge and appreciation of alternate ways of life.

A civilization that cannot accommodate a variety of traditions, seeking to maintain a jealous hold on only one single tradition, can hardly be called a civilization.

The vitality of a religion depends on a continuous critique of it by its own reflective members.

The Indian intelligentsia has somewhat mixed attitudes towards the Indian village. While educated Indians are inclined to think or at least speak well of the village, they do not show much inclination for the company of villagers.

In the past, Indian society was unique in the extremes to which it carried the principle and practice of inequality; today Indian intellectuals appear unique in their zeal for promoting the adoption of equality in every sphere of society.

The striking thing in India is that the extravagant statements made by politicians about the need to end inequality are so widely echoed by our public intellectuals who are nothing if not self-consciously virtuous. These extravagant statements divert attention away from more modest objectives such as controlling poverty, hunger, malnutrition, ill-health and illiteracy, and eliminating the more egregious forms of hierarchical distinction that pervade our public institutions. But that perhaps is what they are meant to do.

Indians . . . tend to write passionately if not stridently; but whether it is academic prose or judicial prose, the passion is often only a thin cover for the weakness of the argument.

I think I have quoted enough to make it clear that the reader is about to make an extended acquaintance with a learned and profoundly humane scholar. For while *Ideology and Social Science* may have begun life as a series of newspaper articles, its contents are of an enduring relevance. They speak to our past and future, as well as our present. There are certainly more passionate books about modern India available in the market. There may even be a few books that are, in a purely factual sense, more informative. But surely none that are wiser.

I
Ideology and Social Science

Teaching and research in the social sciences began in a small way in our universities about a hundred years ago. They expanded greatly after independence with the opening of many new universities and the establishment of specialized institutes of research in the different parts of the country. The work done in them has both broadened and deepened our understanding of economy, society and polity through careful and systematic enquiry and investigation.

The best studies in these disciplines are those that look at the facts in an objective and unbiased way. However, in the study of society and politics it is difficult to do this in a consistent way, and ideological biases creep in. While it is impossible to eliminate biases altogether where the study of human beings is concerned, they are sometimes introduced deliberately as a part of an ideological baggage. While 'left' intellectuals have contributed much to the understanding of our society and history, they have also contributed to the distortion of that understanding by adhering, consciously or unconsciously, to the Leninist dictum that 'those who are not for us are against us'. The essays in this section plead for detachment and objectivity as against partisanship in the study of society.

1

Alternative Sciences

There has been growing disquiet among scientists and scholars in India over the move to introduce astrology and other Vedic sciences in the universities. On the other side, it has been observed that if the social sciences, which lack precision and predictive power, can be taught in universities, there can be no reason for opposing the teaching of astrology. Apart from showing a complete ignorance of the nature and significance of modern science and scholarship, such observations raise fundamental doubts about the viability of the university system in India.

Astrology has its supporters among gifted individuals all over the world, but that does not place it on par with physics, botany, geology, economics or history. It has been pointed out that some of the great Indian mathematicians of the past, such as Aryabhatta and Varahamihira, practised astrology. That is no doubt true. It is also true that Newton devoted much time and energy to the pursuit of alchemy; but that will not be accepted as an argument for introducing alchemy as a subject of study in Cambridge today. What is worrying is not so much the teaching of astrology or alchemy as the ease with which nationalist sentiment can be exploited in India for proposing alternatives to modern systems of knowledge.

The Times of India, 31 July 2001.

The growth of modern knowledge has followed a highly uneven course. It has not taken much account of questions of justice between nations. There is no doubt that India was in advance of the West in many branches of formal knowledge, such as mathematics and grammar, over long periods of history. For several centuries a long line of Indian mathematicians from Brahmagupta to Bhaskaracharya made great advances in their discipline. This may not have been known by their contemporaries in all parts of the world because in the past knowledge was diffused very slowly and with many distortions.

In course of time, India lost its pre-eminence in mathematical science. The mathematicians who flourished in the European centres of learning from the middle of the seventeenth century were largely unaware of the genealogies of their respective disciplines. It is unlikely that Newton and Leibnitz knew about the achievements of their great Indian predecessors or that they wilfully ignored those achievements. It will be perverse to turn our backs on the achievements of modern science on the ground that our own achievements were largely ignored by those who laid the foundations of that science outside India.

The starting point for the advance of modern knowledge is the knowledge at the disposal of the immediately preceding generation. Traditions in science and scholarship are built up by linking one generation to the next, and not by scanning the past in search of distinguished ancestors. The present search for nuggets of wisdom in Vedic science has little to do with the advancement of knowledge; it is driven by a false and atavistic sense of national pride.

Science has now become international in a way in which it was not in the ancient or medieval world. Physicists and mathematicians the world over work with those among the available concepts, methods and theories that are the most useful for their work, without much thought to where they were first devised. In the world as it is, scientists who work in the metropolitan centres in the West enjoy many advantages, and those who work in the peripheries outside the West suffer from many disadvantages. But those disadvantages cannot be overcome by devising fictitious genealogies or by reinventing through fruitless labour what is already available and in use. Raman, Saha and Bose have given enough evidence of the capacity of Indians to contribute fruitfully to modern science for their successors to have to chase the phantoms of the past.

The more able and far-sighted among our scientists will continue the work of their immediate predecessors in India and outside without being seriously diverted by the temptations of astrology, alchemy and Vedic science. If conditions are made too difficult for them in India, they will continue their work outside India. It is simply too wasteful of time and energy for the working physicist or mathematician to turn to Vedic science for inspiration and guidance in his everyday teaching and research. Official interference will act only as an irritant; it cannot reverse the direction given to scientific work in India by several generations of dedicated scientists in our universities and research institutes.

The real threat from atavistic nationalism is to the human sciences and not the natural sciences. Social and political theory are much more vulnerable than physics or mathematics to the demand for creating an alternative science for India. The counterparts of astrology and alchemy in the social sciences are not easy to isolate or immunize. It is too late to convince physical scientists in India that their work will benefit if they begin anew where Vedic science left off. But there are social and political theorists who are ready to be convinced that their work will gain in depth and relevance if they abandon the apparatus of 'Western' in favour of 'Indian' systems of knowledge. In India, the idea of an alternative science is the creation of social and not natural scientists.

The social sciences are more difficult to insulate from ideology and popular prejudice than are the natural sciences. Modern social science, with its roots in nineteenth-century Europe, is a target of attack not only from traditionalists but also from post-modernists. Indian social scientists are very conscious of being latecomers in their fields. Again, they are easily demoralized by the fact that even their genuine contributions are largely ignored outside India. And of course they have never produced a Raman, a Saha or a Bose.

The attack on post-Enlightenment modernity may not always have the intention of reinforcing atavistic nationalism, but it is bound to have that consequence. The post-modernists may not know what they are for, but they know what they are against. The traditionalists are against the same sort of thing, and they do know what they are for: they are for a return to the wisdom of the past. That wisdom has had some attraction for modern social and political theorists in India, several of whom believe that the kernel of their science may be found in the Hindu shastras. The late Professor Kewal Motwani, who greatly admired Manu, maintained that Dharmashastra was the Sanskrit word for sociology. The threat to modern knowledge from astrology and alchemy can be bypassed more easily than the threat to it from Manuvad.

2

Sociology and Ideology

Sociology, as the empirical and systematic study of society and its institutions, is now widely practised in our universities and independent centres of research. It entered the university system in India in the 1920s, barely two or three decades after its adoption by universities in the West. Its spread in India was at first slow. The real growth began after independence, and India now has more sociologists than most countries. At the same time, the growth has been uneven, partly because of the pressures of ideology.

As a result of the work of several generations of sociologists, both Indian and foreign, we now have a fairly detailed knowledge of the social organization of village, caste and family, although our understanding of modern institutions remains sketchy and superficial. Most sociologists would agree in principle that theirs is a comparative science devoted to the understanding of all societies, but in practice Indian sociologists have concentrated almost entirely on the study of their own society.

There are both practical and ideological reasons for the concentration of attention on Indian society to the exclusion of other societies. As I said, sociology began to expand in India around the time of independence, and Indian sociologists

The Telegraph, 3 January 2004.

felt a special responsibility to contribute to the understanding of their society at a turning point in its history. But the neglect of the study of other societies is detrimental to the long-term growth of sociology as an intellectual discipline. It tends to make its practitioners short-sighted and narrow-minded. Our understanding of our own society gains in richness and depth when we compare and contrast it with other societies. It is a cause for worry when virtually every Indian sociologist chooses to be an Indianist rather than a sociologist.

It is natural to expect that the contributions made by sociology will serve a wider public purpose. Some believe that a more informed understanding of how a society works is itself of long-term benefit to its members. Others would like to take the matter further and argue for a more direct role for the sociologist in social and political intervention. Sociologists in India and other recently independent countries seek a more activist and interventionist role for themselves than their counterparts do in countries where the discipline has been established longer.

Sociology has to be distinguished from ideology. Its main aim is the pursuit of systematic knowledge whereas the main aim of ideology is the transformation of society through the pursuit and exercise of power. Of course, no ideologue would like to act blindly, in ignorance of the operation of social and political processes. But in the end, the pursuit of systematic knowledge becomes subordinated to the pursuit of power. Ideologies make large promises to their adherents, but they also demand great sacrifices from them. The most important sacrifice from the intellectual point of view is the sacrifice of individual judgement for a larger political cause in the name of a class, a nation or some other collective entity.

Marxism was the pre-eminent ideology of the twentieth century. Its founder was a man of immense knowledge and analytical skill who set out to discover the laws governing the economic, political and spiritual processes of life. If orthodoxy is a key element in any ideology, then Marx's ideas began to crystallize into an ideology soon after his death. The success of the Bolshevik Revolution turned the ideology into an official doctrine with enormous authority both within and outside the Soviet Union. Individual judgement yielded to political conformity, and Marxist ideology acted as a drug on some of the ablest and most acute minds even when they were outside the reach of the Soviet state.

Sociology has had an uneasy relationship with Marxism since the end of the nineteenth century. This is seen most clearly in Russia where Plekhanov, widely regarded as the father of Russian Marxism, took a hostile attitude to the work of Mikhailovsky with whom sociology made a beginning in Russia; later, Lenin made short work of the young Sorokin who migrated to the United States where he acquired renown as a sociologist at Harvard. After Marxism became established as the official doctrine, little room was left for sociology in the Soviet Union and in countries under its hegemony. Many persons there felt, perhaps sincerely, that there was no need for a separate science of society since all useful knowledge about its nature and operation had been incorporated in dialectical materialism known to millions of school children as Diamat.

Marxism is not the only ideology with which sociology as an empirical and comparative science has to contend. In many parts of the world, including India, nationalism has emerged as a more powerful ideological force than Marxism. In some places and times, Marxism has combined very effectively with nationalism; in others, nationalism has taken over some of the ideological spaces vacated by Marxism. As an ideology, nationalism seeks to develop and promote a unified and idealized image of the nation, and to direct enquiries into the past, present and future conditions of its people in the light of that image. National tradition assumes increasing importance as a standard of evaluation, and any kind of social enquiry that questions or disregards it becomes suspect.

Directing sociological enquiry by the light of national tradition is not a simple matter. There are several national traditions, each casting its light in a particular direction. Not only are different societies heirs to different national traditions, but it is a mistake to believe that each of them is heir to only one single or unitary tradition. What is distinctive of the modern world is not the insulation of different traditions but their interpenetration. It is this that presents to the comparative study of societies its most difficult challenge as well as its most fruitful opportunity.

The nationalist who is consistent in his ideological commitment sets little store by a science of society that seeks to treat all societies or all social traditions alike without bias or prejudice. Treating all societies alike is only an ideal of comparative sociology which, to be sure, is nowhere fully realized in practice. It is well known that the discipline has a Eurocentric bias which goes back to its origins in the nineteenth century when most if not all sociologists were Europeans. That bias is less marked today if only because there are now many non-Western sociologists who study societies throughout the world in broadly the same sort of way. The Western bias in contemporary sociology cannot be wished out of existence, but it is bound to become diluted as more sociologists from outside the West contribute to the general stock of sociological concepts, methods and theories.

There is by now a large accumulation of work on Indian society by both Indian and foreign scholars. It will be futile to turn one's back on this work in the hope of creating a new and distinct sociology for India out of ingredients embedded in Indian traditions of thought. Many Indian sociologists have recommended such a venture for several decades, but few have worked at it with much purpose or determination. The nationalist alternative to sociology has produced very little of substance in any country, far less by any reasonable standard than the Marxist alternative to it.

Myth and History

Twenty years ago, one of our more exuberant public intellectuals introduced a collection of his own essays by saying, 'I shall not grudge it if some enterprising reviewer finds unconvincing history in the following pages, as long as he finds in them convincing myths.' As I read those words, my stomach turned a little. The declaration of preference for myth over history by a recognized social scientist made me wonder when the pigeons would come home to roost. They are now coming home to roost.

Historians and social scientists do not produce myths. At best, they provide the raw materials from which others produce them. Those who provide the raw materials for the production of myths are rarely able to anticipate the form the finished product will take. It is often far removed from the dreams of the providers of raw materials.

What makes a myth convincing is different from what makes history or social science convincing. Myths cannot be subjected to the same test of evidence to which history and social science must submit. It is this freedom from the test of evidence that appeals most to some of our public intellectuals, and their tribe is increasing.

The myth by which increasing numbers of Indians are now

The Telegraph, 11 October 2003.

willing or even eager to be convinced is the myth of national greatness and glory. It is a seductive myth but, like all myths, it simplifies the reality and shows scant respect for contradictory evidence. It is far from my argument that historians or social scientists should not be patriotic, but they should not distort or disregard the facts of the case. The difference between history and myth is that in history, where the facts are unavailable, the argument must rest without a conclusion, whereas a myth must move to its inevitable conclusion, so where there are no facts, they have to be invented.

The natural inclination of teachers of history in India, particularly school teachers, is towards what may be called 'edifying history' as against 'objective' or 'positive' or 'scientific' history. Talking about the greatness and glory of a nation is the easiest way of teaching history—or sociology—in an edifying way to the young. It is easier to do this for the past than for the present so that teachers of sociology have a harder job than teachers of history, particularly ancient history where the facts are vague, unclear and amenable to divergent interpretations. In India teachers do not like relating unpleasant facts to the young, unless the unpleasant facts are about other people.

Indian civilization has great achievements to its credit. Why should teachers of history be loath to talk about them to their students? It is indeed their duty to talk about these achievements provided they take care to avoid too much exaggeration and embellishment. Distortion begins when the teacher turns the spotlight only on the achievements of his nation and always away from its failings. There is no civilization that has only achievements and no failings. The natural tendency in nationalist myth-making is to embellish the achievements of the nation and to brush its failings under the carpet.

Perhaps the majority of teachers would like to say to their students that India is a great country and, as I have suggested, there is no harm in this provided some moderation is maintained. Some go on from there to say that India is not just great, it is the greatest, and it is at this point that the falsification begins. It is of course difficult to maintain that India is the greatest in its present state, but one may, with a little effort, persuade oneself and others that it was the greatest in its pristine state. For the teacher who is a zealous nationalist, history has more possibilities than sociology.

The glory begins with the land. India has, of course, been represented in song as a land overflowing with milk and honey, and this is true of many other countries as well. The question is, how far what is commemorated in song should be taken as the literal truth to be taught to students through textbooks of history and social studies. In a recent book, written for a wide readership, India is represented as having the best of everything: the best of sunshine and rainfall, the best rivers and mountains, an abundance of every form of plant and animal life, and, of course, inexhaustible stores of all the necessities of everyday life.

In this representation, the country's most valued resource is its traditional social life, animated by tolerance, forbearance, fortitude, compassion and all the other virtues that made India the envy of the rest of the civilized world. The privileged site of these virtues was the Indian village community where peace, prosperity and goodwill among men prevailed. Reading all this, one would get hardly any idea of the divisions of caste, the practice of untouchability or the subordination of women; and the representation is completely at odds with Dr Ambedkar's depiction of the Indian village as 'a sink of localism, a den of ignorance, narrow-mindedness and communalism'.

Dr Ambedkar notwithstanding, more and more students are being taught by their teachers about the greatness and glory of India. After learning so much about India's pristine condition, some of them might wish to know why there is so much poverty, inequality and discord in India today. Why is India's present so completely different from its past? Those who read the edifying textbooks also read newspapers and watch television, and it is difficult to reconcile the messages that come from these different sources.

There is an obvious and attractive explanation for the mismatch between the splendour of the past and the squalor of the present, and that is the intervention of colonial rule. The same textbooks that represent the India of the past as a land overflowing with milk and honey also represent colonial rule as a period of relentless plunder, spoliation and degradation. Myths have need not only of the forces of light but also of the forces of darkness. In the last few decades, the best liberal and radical historians have trained their heaviest guns against the misdeeds of colonial rule to which all of India's present ills are attributed. This monotonically anti-colonial historiography has made it easy for the traditionalists to represent India's past as a period of glory and grandeur.

The British were no doubt alien intruders who disrupted a contented and harmonious way of life. But were they the first or only intruders to do so? What our radical and liberal historians have started is being continued further back into the past by other historians. A recent account of the pristine greatness of India and its spoliation by the British ends by saying that perhaps the gloom had set in earlier, around AD 1000. Who were the bearers of this pre-British gloom? Could they have been Afghans, or Turks? The myth of the destruction of everything that was good in India by the British has extensions that may not all be pleasing to those who have contributed to its making. But the creators of myths do not expect to be asked to take responsibility for their creations.

Teaching and Research

India's poor record in literacy and primary education is nothing short of a scandal. Despite the many problems with which it started at independence, a country with India's material and intellectual resources could have done better. It is not that good intentions were entirely lacking. The constitution made the provision of free and compulsory education up to the age of fourteen a directive principle of state policy, but decades after its adoption even literacy was absent in more than half the population. Higher education received a larger share of public attention in the early years of independence.

Things have begun to change. On the positive side, there is greater public awareness of the importance of elementary education, and a stronger sense of urgency in making it universal. Matters are no longer left in the hands of the government only. Companies, NGOs and even international agencies have begun to play a part in reaching primary education to all. By contrast, the universities as centres of higher education have now entered a phase of decline. Government funding is drying up, and little if any private benefaction is flowing in.

The public attitude towards the universities has undergone

---

a sea-change. India's first prime minister cared for the universities in a way in which few heads of government anywhere in the world do today. In a memorable convocation address delivered in Allahabad a few months after independence, Nehru had said, 'If the universities discharge their duties adequately, it is well with the nation and the people.' He expected the universities to make a significant contribution to the new awakening in India to which many looked forward at that time.

Things are not well with the universities today. For every ten persons who will speak up for primary education, there is hardly one who will speak up for the university, unless he has a personal interest in a post or a promotion. But if we disregard higher education now, there will be in the future the same cause for regret that there has been over the neglect of primary education in the past. India needs an effective system of higher education as much as it needs an extensive system of primary education. Nothing can be more shallow than the view that in a poor country primary education deserves public support whereas higher education can take care of itself. They both need public support and sympathy.

The universities owe much of their present predicament to their own improvident and thriftless ways. In the 1950s and 1960s, academic entrepreneurs embarked on a course of reckless expansion of staff and students in the name of planning and development. Then the initiative passed to the teachers' unions which succeeded in browbeating the authorities into relaxing academic standards in the name of equity and social justice. By the 1990s, universities all over the country had become noisy and disorderly places with very little to show for themselves by way of academic performance.

Nevertheless, teaching and research have not died out in the Indian universities, and they still meet an important social need, although not quite in the way in which Nehru had hoped. A country like India depends for its progress, and even its survival, on modern knowledge, and the universities play a vital part in the production and transmission of that knowledge. For all their failings, they have contributed significantly to the modernization of India in the last hundred years. They were among the first open and secular institutions in the country, and they provided not only a new type of knowledge but also a new social setting for interchange between men and women from different castes and communities, and also from different regions.

Their open nature makes universities particularly vulnerable to exposure and pressure. Pressure on the universities has been mounting steadily in recent years. The most irksome form in which it comes is advice to make the work of the universities more relevant to the needs of society. Much of the advice is shallow and uninformed, but advice from those who wield authority or control funds is difficult to ignore. When the universities are doing well in their own sphere, which is the pursuit of science and scholarship, they can deal with gratuitous advice on their own terms; because they are not doing well now, they can be easily unsettled by being told that their work is not socially relevant.

Programmes to inject more relevance into the work of the universities take different forms. They are not all subversive of the academic objectives of the universities, but many of them are even when their promoters act from good intentions. The two most popular sorts of programmes are those that seek to enhance the earning capacities of university graduates and those that seek to improve their moral standing.

Universities are not best suited to providing vocational training; they were not designed to do so. But under the threat of financial cuts from the government, postgraduate departments are now turning their attention to courses of study and research that appear to offer immediate financial returns. From this point of view, work in basic disciplines such as philosophy, history and mathematics, which promises little immediate return, appears to be socially unproductive. Yet neglect of study and research in the basic arts and sciences cannot but lead to the depletion of society's intellectual capital in the long run. The problem is compounded by the fact that many heads of universities themselves feel that their institutions should be made to appear attractive from the commercial point of view.

The very people who wish to make the universities more attractive commercially also wish them to be more active in promoting moral values. Recent attempts by the ministry of human resource development to introduce value education (VE) into university curricula has caused concern among serious academics. Some believe that the guidelines are part of a plot to introduce Hindutva into higher education through the back door. My own conclusion, after a careful examination of the relevant documents, is that they are the work of amiable cranks who have convinced themselves that they have solved the problem of good and evil. It is only because the Indian university is so weak and vulnerable that one has to worry about what can be done to it by determined ideologues or well-meaning cranks in positions of power.

The modern university is based on the ideal of the unity of teaching and research. The quality of research in the Indian university is highly uneven. The distractions arising from the search for commercial advantage and moral benefit will hasten the decline that has already set in. In the social sciences there is already a diversion of funds from the universities to organizations that are prepared to undertake projects and produce reports efficiently and expeditiously. Part of the

climate in India. Each of them stood for modernity in his own time and advocated modernization in his own way, although this is not to say that all their ideas are relevant or useful today. The current attack on Macaulay and Marx is an attack on modern ideas, although those who engage in it are not always aware of the roots or the implications of their resentment of the modern world.

Both Macaulay and Marx had powerful minds which produced many seminal ideas. But they belonged to the nineteenth century and neither of them was fully free from the prejudices common to Europeans of their age. Their views would today be considered Eurocentric by the standards of fair-minded intellectuals even in the West, not to speak of India.

Nothing would be more thoughtless than to accept their views on India—or any other subject—*in toto* or uncritically. But a wholesale and uncritical rejection of what they stood for and sought to promote would be a step in the wrong direction.

Marx's ideas became very influential after his death and Marxism acquired a life of its own in the twentieth century. It took different forms in the different parts of the world and it also changed over time, becoming very rigid in some places at certain times and quite flexible in other places at other times. Marxism influenced all intellectual disciplines in the humanities and the social sciences, and it came to be called the Latin of the twentieth century. Even those who were resolutely opposed to it could not escape its influence so long as they kept their minds open and active.

From the very beginning Marxism has had a liberal as well as a dogmatic tendency, and the interplay of these two tendencies may be seen in Marx's own life and work. Apologists for Marxism have argued that its dogmatic tendencies were aberrations, but that has carried little conviction with those who have been victims of Marxist sectarianism and partisanship. Marxist dogmatism has not been confined only to matters of the mind, and it has not always been inoffensive. Marxists have used state power to protect ideological purity, and official patronage to promote intellectual mediocrity. But they have not been in power everywhere or always, and not all of them have sought power or patronage. In any case, it will be safe to say that one need not be a Marxist in order to draw from the storehouse of Marxian ideas.

The political fortunes of Marxism have varied between countries and fluctuated over time. In India, as in most parts of the world, it is now in a phase of decline rather than ascendancy. But that does not mean that it can be written off intellectually. Indeed, intellectually Marxism has generally fared better when Marxists were out of power than when they were in power. And in India at least, they are better equipped intellectually than their adversaries in the present political and academic establishments at the centre.

Today while there are many, including some very able intellectuals, who will stand up for Marx, there are few, if any, who will stand up for Macaulay. This is remarkable because the modern Indian intelligentsia as a whole has been shaped by an educational and a legal system in whose creation Macaulay had played some part. If it be said that he had made uninformed and ill-judged statements about the Indian intellectual tradition, it can hardly be maintained that Marx had painted a very flattering picture of Indian society and culture. Left intellectuals are unwilling to give Macaulay the benefit of doubt that they are only too eager to give to Marx. Yet we may well ask what kind of left intellectuals we would have today without the reforms introduced by Macaulay and others into India in the nineteenth century.

When it comes to assessing the part played by colonial rule in the reordering of Indian society and culture, there appears to be little to choose between left and right intellectuals. Giving colonial rule its due share of praise in the making of modern India is not politically correct for the one any more than it is for the other. Here left intellectuals are similar to their counterparts on the right and different from Marx. For all the vitriol that he poured on individual members of the British ruling class, Marx had the discernment to recognize that that class was the historical agent of a change for the better in Indian society, and also that no major change comes without a price tag.

The making of modern India which began under colonial rule was not a painless process. Indians who participated in it from the middle of the nineteenth century to the middle of the twentieth had to swallow many bitter pills. But on the whole they acted with dignity and restraint. They did not strike unnecessary postures and they owned responsibility for the many evils that had accumulated in their society. Above all, they were willing to learn from their colonial masters even when the latter might appear odious and reprehensible as persons. It is this that makes the best among the nationalist leaders stand out as superior, intellectually and morally, to the custodians of imperial rule.

More than fifty years after independence, our attitudes towards the changes introduced under colonial rule have altered. Marxists, subalternists, feminists, nationalists and revivalists vie with each other to bring out the horrors of colonial rule. All the social evils with which we are still grappling, including the excesses of caste and patriarchy, are traced back to that period in our history. In this kind of intellectual climate Macaulay becomes a soft target in comparison with Marx, or even the madrasas. Whatever we might think of Macaulay, we should never forget that in the nineteenth century he opened a window for us on to the modern world, and if we shut that window now, it will be at our cost and not his.

6

Wages of Partisanship

The previous government under Mr Atal Bihari Vajpayee has some achievements to its credit, but its interventions in the fields of education and research will not be counted among them. It is not simply that the ministry of human resource development acted badly, but the principles under which it acted were wrong. It adopted a distinct ideology and sought to direct education and research by its light, rewarding those who conformed to it and disregarding, if not penalizing, those who did not. Inevitably, a network of patronage came into operation. This may be seen in the ways in which it set about rewriting school textbooks and reconstituting institutions of social science research. Many felt that the attitudes to education and culture prevalent in the ministry were backward rather that forward looking.

The free development of knowledge is harmed when a government or a party uses the institutions of education and research to promote its own ideology. This is true irrespective of the nature of the ideology, whether it is conservative or radical, of the right or of the left. The misdeeds of the last government should serve as an object lesson to those who believe that there is no harm in putting science and scholarship in the service of ideology, provided it is the right kind of

The Telegraph, 5 August 2004.

ideology. For it cannot be denied that there are intellectuals, including able and well-meaning ones, who believe that science and scholarship gain and do not lose when they are driven by ideology. Sooner or later they become partisans in the service of one political formation or another.

The problem is especially acute in the social and cultural sciences such as history, sociology and political science, and it operates to some extent independently of the good or evil designs of the government in office. Social scientists have divided opinions on the desirability of allowing their preferred social and political values to guide their teaching and research. Some of them are in favour of detachment, objectivity and value-neutrality, while others favour commitment and engagement. Those who advocate commitment to one or another set of social and political values are more likely than the others to slip into partisanship in their teaching and research.

In a democratic order, where groups with rival policies and programmes contend for public support, partisanship is the normal and expected course in the political arena. It does not follow that it is either necessary or desirable in institutions of education and research. It is essential to distinguish between those spheres of society in which partisanship is legitimate or even desirable and those in which it is not, instead of taking the same position on it across the board.

The sociologist Max Weber, who was an advocate of value-neutral social science, made this point in his observations on Heinrich Treitschke, one of the most popular German historians of his time. Treitschke was a strong advocate of nationalism and an opponent of socialism, and he used his university chair freely to propagate his political views. Weber's objection to this was not based on any antipathy to nationalism or sympathy for socialism, but simply on the view that a professor should not put scholarship in the service of ideology in the classroom. He was free to use a political platform to propagate his political views, but his obligation as a teacher was to always present both sides of a case, objectively and impartially, before his students. In teaching and research, unlike in politics, fair-mindedness rather than partisanship is the superior value. One should preach neither nationalism nor socialism in the classroom; there are other places where one is free to do that.

What is wrong with the ideology of Hindu nationalism? One might well say that it is based on the values of a great and ancient civilization, values that are accommodative, pluralistic and tolerant. Why should the propagation of Hindu nationalism through teaching and research be viewed with mistrust? No matter how great or glorious a national tradition might be, it has its dark side, and therefore the tradition as a whole must be examined in a critical spirit. No doubt the Indian social tradition was tolerant in comparison with other social traditions, but it tolerated the practice of untouchability and the perpetual tutelage of women.

The glorification of national tradition acquires a new momentum when it enters the agenda of a political party and when that party in turn assumes political office. Then watchdogs are put in place to ensure that the national tradition is 'correctly' represented with all the dark patches gradually effaced. The work of the scholar and the teacher, which is to reveal the light as well as the shadows, is corrupted. There are always enough compliant intellectuals and bureaucrats to serve as watchdogs, and some of them become more zealous than their political masters. The outcome is that a complex and contradictory reality is simplified in order to meet partisan ends; simplification leads to distortion, and distortion to falsification.

It will be a mistake to believe that simplification,

distortion and falsification for partisan ends is confined only to nationalist ideologies or ideologies of the right. Partisanship in the cause of socialism or in left-wing causes in a broader sense has been common and widespread. Such partisanship has been justified in the fields of teaching and research by the argument that the materialist interpretation of history provides the only scientific basis for the understanding of economic, political and social reality. The classic statement of the case may be found in the writings of Lenin. 'Marx and Engels', he wrote, 'were partisans in philosophy from start to finish, they were able to detect the deviations from materialism and concessions to fideism in every one of the "recent" trends.' Generations of Soviet and other East European students were fed on textbooks permeated by the distortions and falsifications that resulted from Lenin's call for partisanship. There is a tendency in some of these countries now to go to the opposite extreme to rectify the distortions of the past.

Partisans for the materialist interpretation of history have never had in India the kind of free hand with textbooks that they had in the USSR. At the same time, where left intellectuals have had power and influence, they have not been shy to use them for partisan ends. They have been self-righteous and intellectually arrogant, attacking the evils of Western capitalism mercilessly while turning a blind eye to the horrors of Soviet socialism. And in the same partisan spirit, they have promoted second-rate and worse than second-rate scholars and teachers on the ground that they had the correct ideological orientation.

Some of the damage done to education and research by the thoughtless partisanship of the previous regime will no doubt be corrected. But there are right ways and wrong ways for intellectuals to deal with the problem. The wrong way would be for them to approach the government to help them to go back to the days when left intellectuals ruled the roost. Very little will be gained if one kind of partisanship is replaced by another. The autonomy of intellectual life must be restored, but that cannot be done unless intellectuals recognize that partisanship in any political cause subverts the pursuit of learning.

II
Religion, Language and Culture

Religion is an important part of our society, hence an important subject of study for the social sciences. The social scientist treats religion with respect but his perspective on it is different from that of the religious believer. He recognizes that religious beliefs, practices and symbols unite people but sees that they divide them as well. Hence he studies religion as a source of cohesion and also as a source of conflict. His main task is to examine, interpret and analyse religion as it actually operates and not as it is supposed to operate. Above all, he tries as far as possible not to take sides between the different religious faiths.

Language too is a source of both cohesion and conflict in any country where there are many languages and not just several religions. Many Indians, including those who have little formal education, are at ease with more than one language, and this is an invaluable asset for us. Sometimes people develop a jealous attitude towards their own language and argue as if it cannot grow unless English is abolished from our schools and colleges. This is a retrograde attitude and acts against the long-term interest of both democracy and development. While religion and language constitute important ingredients of culture, they do not exhaust the whole of it. Some of the essays in this section deal with certain general features of contemporary Indian culture in the face of modernity.

7

Religion and Society

Just over fifty years ago, M.N. Srinivas, who was to emerge as India's leading sociologist, published his book *Religion and Society among the Coorgs of South India*. The book introduced a new approach to the understanding of Hinduism, and it established its author's reputation as a sociologist of the first rank. In it he used the distinction between the book-view and the field-view of society and the contrast between the Indological and the sociological approaches to religion. It may appear in retrospect that the contrast was overdrawn; but it expressed an insight of great significance.

Srinivas became the leading advocate of the field-view and the sociological approach, by which he meant an approach based on a careful and methodical examination of observed or observable facts. It does not treat religion as being either completely autonomous or as invariant, eternal and unchanging. Religious beliefs and practices vary and change, and this has to be examined in relation to variation and change in the structure of society. No religion operates independently of specific social arrangements, and Srinivas set out to show the two-way relationship between religion and social structure. This approach does not always find favour with religious believers who are inclined to regard religion as pure and society as corrupt.

The Telegraph, 13 February 2003.

The believer seeks out what he sees as the invariant and unchanging core of religion, and when he does not find it, he tends to put the blame on external material and historical forces for it. The Hindus in particular have lived with the idea of Kaliyuga since time immemorial, and that has helped them to explain many things away. The sociologist, on the other hand, recognizes that religious beliefs and practices are embedded in the social order, and tries to see how they are refracted by it. For him, Hinduism is not single and indivisible. Thus, Srinivas spoke of local Hinduism, regional Hinduism, peninsular Hinduism and all-India Hinduism. He also showed how religious beliefs and practices were refracted by the structures of joint family, caste and village.

Srinivas drew pointed attention to the limitations of the book-view of Hinduism which was the view accepted by most educated Hindus at the time. By the book-view of Hinduism he meant that view of it which was based on an understanding of ancient and medieval texts. He believed that those texts were remote from the current reality and that they gave a false sense of unity and harmony whereas the actual beliefs and practices of the Hindus were full of ambiguity and inconsistency. This was true not only of religion but also of major social institutions such as caste and joint family. The field-view would bring the reality closer to the understanding of educated Indians.

Historically speaking, the sociological approach to religion advocated by Srinivas is an offspring of religious scepticism rather than religious faith. Moreover, it is of relatively recent origin. Even in the West, it is scarcely a hundred years old. Today the sociology of religion is a well-established discipline in the West, but, despite the lead given by Srinivas more than fifty years ago, it is not so in India.

In the Western countries the sociology of religion faced stiff opposition at first from the practitioners of established disciplines such as theology and the philosophy of religion. The theologians mistrusted the moral detachment with which the sociologists sought to approach their subject. When they examined Christianity on the same plane of observation and analysis as other religions such as Hinduism or even animism, they were denounced for denigrating the true faith. The sociology of religion, on the other hand, is concerned with neither the denigration nor the adulation of any particular religion but with examining the varieties of religious beliefs and practices in their specific social contexts.

For the believer, religion is the most important part of social life. For the sociologist, there are also other important features of it, such as kinship, economics and politics, and he tries to show how religion is related to them. Not only is the sociologist reluctant to assign a privileged place to religion among the various institutions of society, he is also reluctant to assign a privileged place to any one religion as against the rest.

When Srinivas published his study of the Coorgs shortly after independence, he did not have to face the kind of opposition from established religious positions that his predecessors in the West had had to face fifty years or so before him. The climate of opinion in Nehru's India was more tolerant of religious scepticism and even religious dissent. At the same time, the lead given by Srinivas in the objective and empirical study of Hinduism was not followed by many sociologists in India. Where it comes to religion, the approach of the moralist prevails over that of the sociologist, at least among Indians, including Indian sociologists. The moralist tends either to extol religion—true religion as he perceives it—as the cure for every ill, or to condemn it as false consciousness or the opium of the masses.

It is a difficult thing for believing and practising Hindus to examine their own religion objectively and dispassionately. But unless this is done we will not be able to see clearly the inner contradictions of Hinduism that a changing social and political order is bringing to the surface. Hindu intellectuals responded better to the challenge that their religion faced in the early phase of colonial rule than their counterparts are doing today.

A distinction is now increasingly being made between Hindutva and Hinduism. Hindutva has adopted an aggressive posture and its proponents wish to create a Hindu state, presumably along lines similar to the Islamic republic of Pakistan. Liberal Hindus are appalled by the aggressiveness, but their intellectual response can hardly be regarded as adequate. They reject Hindutva, but they cannot turn their backs on Hinduism. They invoke a tolerant and benevolent form of Hinduism which is presumed to have prevailed before it was appropriated by evil and vengeful persons for their own nefarious ends.

It is true that, on a certain plane, Hinduism has a remarkable tradition of tolerance. It is no less true that it has a remarkable tradition of hierarchy. The tradition of tolerance included the tolerance of untouchability and the perpetual tutelage of women. It is easy enough, while talking about Hinduism, to move on to the lofty plane of pluralistic values and to ignore the social consequences of the hierarchical structure of those values.

The hierarchy operated, and to some extent continues to operate, through the most elaborate and comprehensive forms of social exclusion known to human history. Social exclusion was maintained through the rules of purity and pollution which have deep roots in Hindu religion. It is to Srinivas's credit that he explained the operation of these mechanisms and their central place in the religious life of the Hindus. He always described himself as a Hindu, and it was far from his intention to denigrate his own religion. But as a sociologist, he sought to present a balanced account of it. A balanced account of Hinduism cannot sweep under the carpet the contradiction inherent in it between the principle of accommodation and the principle of hierarchy.

8

Hinduism in Danger?

Some of the most vivid recollections of my childhood go back to the Great Calcutta Killings when as a boy of eleven or twelve I had to travel by bus and tram between home and school in an unsafe city. I did not have a clear understanding of what was happening, but something from those days that echoes in my memory is the phrase 'Islam in danger'.

The phrase had different connotations at home and in the school. At school I came to befriend a number of Muslim boys whose social and political orientations were very different from those of my home. They spoke Urdu and English rather than Bengali. They were a couple of years older than me, took a keen interest in politics and were passionately attached to the idea of Pakistan which in 1946 seemed a fantasy to me. They had obviously been taught at home that in India there was a serious threat not only to the Muslims as a minority but also to Islam as a way of life.

My home environment was quite different. The place where we lived at that time was not my parents' home but one to which my mother, born a Bengali Hindu, was closely attached by ties of fictive kinship. It was a liberal, secular, middle-class Bengali home, strongly attached to the idea of a single India and strongly opposed to the two-nation theory.

The Hindu, 3 January 2003.

The most articulate member of the household, who was a humane and broad-minded nationalist, became my mother's political mentor. I remember him explaining to us with great clarity and conviction that the idea of Islam in danger was wrong and pernicious and that it would bring great suffering to the Muslim minority for whose predicament he had deep and genuine sympathy.

The wheel seems to be turning full circle now, and more and more people are beginning to feel and say that Hinduism is in danger. If someone strongly opposes that view, he may be denounced as a pseudo-secularist, even if he happens to be the prime minister of India. Surely, it is this growing hysteria about the danger to Hinduism that has led members of his own parivar or extended family to describe even the stout-hearted Mr Advani as a pseudo-secularist.

The hysteria about Hinduism in danger is growing and spreading, and it tends to catch liberal and enlightened Hindus on the wrong foot. This seems now to be the most serious challenge not only to the religious minorities but to Indian society as a whole and, indeed, to Hinduism itself. One would expect Hindu intellectuals, whether they are secularists, pseudo-secularists or plain honest Hindus, to oppose the spread of this hysteria which is being nurtured by persons whose main motivation is revenge for real or imagined injuries inflicted on their co-religionists in the past or the present. Yet one sees very little intellectual opposition to it from within Hinduism.

At the time of independence Hindu intellectuals were by and large free from the kind of paranoia that characterized many of their Muslim counterparts, and this continued into the years of Nehru's prime ministership and beyond. But the tide may now be turning. Hindu intellectuals appear less confident about the prospects of a modern, secular and democratic political order in India than they were when the republic came into being in 1950. Some if not many of them have begun to feel that Hinduism is in danger not only from other religions but from secular modernity itself. The attack on pseudo-secularists comes not only from those who are opposed to other religions but also from those who are opposed to secular ideas and institutions.

Is Hinduism really in danger? On the evidence, objectively considered, the presumption will be that Hinduism is far less endangered in independent India than Islam was in India before independence. But that is not really the point, for the objective evidence of danger is one thing and the feeling of being endangered is another. It may well be that the number of Muslims now in Pakistan who feel that Islam is in danger is larger than the number of those who felt in that way in undivided India. The partition of India did not reduce the feeling among Muslims on the subcontinent that Islam was in danger; it probably enhanced it.

Where is the danger to Hinduism believed to come from? Does it come from other religions within or outside the country? Or does it come from the ascendance of secular ideas and institutions which tend to be represented by both Hindu and Muslim traditionalists as godless and immoral?

There has been some agitation in recent times over conversions from Hinduism to other religions. Various things may be said for and against religious conversion. But surely, one is not going to argue that the conversion of a few hundred, or a few thousand, or even a few hundred thousand Hindus to Islam or Christianity or Buddhism will bring about the collapse of an ancient, complex and vibrant religion such as Hinduism. Hinduism has withstood conversion on a far more massive scale in the past. It is most unlikely that conversion on that kind of scale will ever take place in the future.

It is said that Hindus are no longer safe in their own country since their temples are now open to assault. The assault on places of worship of no matter which religion is a criminal act which does not weaken religious faith and observance as much as it challenges the legitimacy of the secular state whose responsibility it is to protect all places of worship.

Acts of competitive vandalism aimed at the desecration of sacred places are on the increase. Sometimes they are undertaken with the open or tacit encouragement of popular religious functionaries. Today it is those who engage in such acts who are likely to raise the slogan that their religion is in danger. But the sad thing is that they are not the only ones. Those who first raised the slogan of Islam in danger in pre-partition India were not all vandals. Some of them were educated, even cultivated men. Indeed, intellectuals always play a part in creating channels for the expression of popular passions. They do not always do so with evil intentions, but they are easily intoxicated by their own ideas when they find that those ideas resonate among the masses of people.

The disquiet about the future of Hinduism seems to be more widespread among Hindu intellectuals than it was fifty years ago. How far this mirrors the disquiet among those who speak for the minority religions, and how far it is based on autonomous and independent causes, it is not easy to determine.

As the strains created in society by secular modernity become increasingly apparent, more and more Hindu intellectuals are beginning to believe that their religion and way of life are endangered. They are less confident about it than they ought to be in view of its demonstrated vitality, resilience and adaptability. One consequence of this is that the internal critique of Hinduism which began in the nineteenth century and continued for well over a hundred years seems to be drying up. This is unfortunate because the vitality of a religion depends upon a continuous critique of it by its own reflective members. Some years ago, the Marxist economist and writer Ashok Rudra published a critique of Hinduism in Bengali entitled *Brahminical Religion and the Mentality of the Modern Hindu*. I wonder how many such books are being written today in Hindi which is the most widely used among the Indian languages.

Enlightened Hindus in the nineteenth century felt free to attack the corruption and decay in their own religion and among their own religious leaders. Their present-day counterparts find it more convenient to train their guns on secular intellectuals than on their own religious leaders whose intolerant and vengeful acts do far greater harm to Hinduism from within. If Hinduism is in danger today, the main source of that danger may lie within and not outside it.

9

Secularism Re-examined

The public debate on secularism is acquiring some curious features. It is obvious that many persons have misgivings about it but, with the exception of a few mavericks, they are generally not prepared to attack it openly. While this is true by and large of the intelligentsia, it is invariably the case with politicians. It would be unthinkable for any political leader, whether of the left or the right, to speak openly against secularism, just as it would be unthinkable for him to speak openly against equality.

The most common way to throw doubt on secularism is for a person to say that he is not against secularism, what he is against is pseudo-secularism. He will then go on to say that there are far too many pseudo-secularist busybodies around, and that they are the ones who are responsible for the discord between communities and, ultimately, for communal violence. I have known professed adherents of Hindutva say that they are for secularism, that Hindutva itself is a form of secularism, indeed its most exalted form, only they prefer to call it religious pluralism rather than secularism which is of Western provenance. Religious pluralism, in their view, is not only a part of the Indian tradition, it is tolerant and undogmatic unlike secularism which has a whiff of dogmatic atheism about it and, besides, lacks moral depth.

The misgiving about secularism, vague and ill-formed by itself, is fed by misgivings about many other things: about atheism, about Marxism, about socialism, and about the modern world. I am convinced that some of the more humane among the adherents of Hindutva would be reconciled with secularism if only it could be rescued from modernity. But it cannot: secularism is a modern and not a traditional value. The religious pluralism—or, if one prefers, the religious tolerance—of the past was rooted in a hierarchical social order in which some communities, together with their beliefs and practices, were regarded as unquestionably superior to others.

Western observers of this country often say that secularism in India is something quite different from what it is in the West. When pressed to explain what they mean, they invariably point to the wide gap between profession and practice. Many Indians do just the same, and some conclude from this that secularism, particularly of the Western kind, no matter how desirable in itself, cannot work in India. The gap between profession and practice is indeed very large, but I doubt that it exists only in India. Even the French, the great paragons of secularism in the West, have been caught on the wrong foot over the use of the veil and the cross in their public schools. Granting that the gap is larger in this country than elsewhere, it does not follow that secularism means one thing outside India and an altogether different thing in India.

Indians who are mistrustful of modernity say that they should be free to develop their own conception of secularism and not be burdened by the Western conception of it. Is there a distinctively Indian conception of the secular, and is it radically different from the Western one? In seeking answers to these questions it is important to avoid being pushed into extreme positions. Obviously the idea of the secular acquires some of the colour of the social environment in which it operates, but that does not mean that it cannot be fruitfully compared—or contrasted—with its counterparts elsewhere. Nor can we say that there is a single, uniform conception of the secular throughout the West. It is true that there is no exact equivalent of the English word 'secular' in any Indian language. But then, as more than one French sociologist has told me, the French word 'laïque', which is used to describe the republic in the Constitution of France, cannot be exactly translated into English. If the idea of the secular varies between India and the West, it also varies between Britain, France and Germany.

I prefer to speak of secularization which is a widespread tendency in the modern world. In India, as elsewhere, it is driven by a variety of forces among which secularism as an ideology is only one. Here I would like to dwell briefly on two distinct forces that contribute to secularization. The first is the compulsion of fairness—or equality—between religious communities in a country where diverse religious faiths co-exist. The second is a process of specialization and differentiation whereby institutions and practices earlier regulated by religious authority and religious doctrine cease to be so regulated. The issue of religious pluralism is directly relevant to only the first and not the second. Specialization and differentiation may lead to secularization even in a society where there is only one single religion.

Shortly after independence India adopted a new constitution providing a charter for a secular state and a secular concept of citizenship. This was dictated above all by the compulsions of history and of demography. A constitution that was the end-product of a nationalist movement that had resolutely opposed the two-nation theory could hardly prescribe a Hindu state or any kind of religious state. For Nehru and his generation, having a secular state was not just a matter of convenience, it was also a matter of honour. And nobody understood the value of a secular conception of citizenship better than Dr Ambedkar.

A secular legal and constitutional order is dictated also by the compulsions of demography. India is a land of many religions, and, within each religion, of many sects and denominations. There are more Muslims in India than in any country in the world save Indonesia, and India's Muslim population is larger than the total population of Britain, France or Germany. There are also populous minorities of Christians and Sikhs. It will be impossible to govern such a country without secular public institutions that treat citizens without fear or favour, irrespective of their religion.

In addition to the compulsions of fairness, secularization is driven also by the requirements of development and modernization. If we wish to have a modern educational system and a modern economic system, we must build secular institutions: secular schools, colleges and universities; secular offices and factories; and secular print and electronic media. M.N. Srinivas had famously defined secularization as follows: 'the term "secularization" implies that what was previously regarded as religious is ceasing to be such, and it also implies a process of differentiation which results in the various aspects of society, economic, political, legal and moral, becoming increasingly *discrete* in relation to each other.' It cannot be too strongly emphasized that differentiation does not mean disconnection.

The differentiation of society is a long-term evolutionary tendency, and India can attempt to reverse that tendency only at its own peril. Secularization does not mean that religious institutions will cease to exist; it only means that they will cease to encompass or regulate all the other institutions of society. These other institutions will then act relatively autonomously in their respective specialized domains, such as those of education, science, finance, administration, communication, and so on.

Some believe that secularism in India is a matter of the equal treatment of all religions whereas in the West it is a matter of differentiation and autonomy from religious regulation and control, and therefore the two are radically different. This is a mistake. Both considerations enter the conception of the secular in India as well as in the West, though perhaps not in the same proportions. The problem of parity between Protestants and Catholics is a serious one in countries such as Germany, Holland and Belgium, not to speak of Northern Ireland; and the urge to develop education, science and scholarship independently of religious regulation and control has been an important social force in India for well over a hundred years. It is necessary and desirable to remain aware of the distinctive constellation of forces that operate in India; but to continuously play the tune of Indian exceptionalism is tedious and unproductive.

10

Secularization of Work

Work is an important part of life in all societies although there are some individuals everywhere who manage to get by without doing very much of it. Societies differ in their organization of work including the division of labour and the ranking of occupations. These are much more rigid and elaborate in some societies than in others. Work practices and norms change, though not as much as one might desire, with changes in technology, in material resources and in the size and density of population, and with the emergence of new ideas, beliefs and values.

Two hundred years ago, Henri de Saint-Simon, who was one of the precursors of socialism, believed that a new type of society, which he called industrial society, was emerging in Europe in which only those who worked would be esteemed unlike in earlier societies in which work was disdained and left to be done by social inferiors. Further, all work that was socially useful and productive would be equally esteemed. Saint-Simon may be regarded as the prophet of the secularization of work. Industrialization did bring about significant changes in work practices and norms, but this does not mean that all occupations are equally esteemed in even the most advanced industrial societies today.

The Telegraph, 6 April 2003.

Indian attitudes to work differ significantly from attitudes even in other Asian countries such as Japan. I had noticed in Osaka that police constables and taxi drivers wore white gloves. I made fun of this to a young Japanese anthropologist who was with me. She put me in my place very politely but effectively. She said, 'In Japan people respect the work they do, even if it is that of a policeman or a taxi driver. In India there is respect only for the well-born and the well-to-do; there is no respect for useful work.' The middle-class Indian's contempt for manual and menial work has no equal anywhere.

In pre-industrial civilizations the allocation of work was governed more or less strictly by ascriptive criteria such as race, caste, creed and sex. Even in simple tribal societies men and women did different kinds of work; women were excluded from some occupations, and others were only for them. The major agrarian civilizations, whether in Europe, India or China, were hierarchical in character, and their populations were divided into estates or castes whose members were not expected to do the same kinds of work. Menial and manual work was left to the lowest strata and there were sanctions against the performance of such work by the well-born and the well-to-do.

In medieval Europe a person belonging to a superior estate might suffer derogation or loss of rank if he habitually engaged in menial work. Loss of rank in medieval Europe was nothing compared to the loss of caste that might follow in India from doing the wrong kind of work. Even fifty years after the adoption of a constitution that guarantees equality and freedom to all, the fear of losing caste, metaphorically if not literally, affects the choice of occupations among middle-class Indians more than among middle-class people elsewhere.

Still, having to lose caste only metaphorically is an improvement on being made to lose it literally. At least among the educated urban middle class, upper-caste Indians no longer need to fear expulsion from caste for adopting occupations whose adoption would have led to such expulsion in the not-too-distant past. Modernization has not solved all problems, but it has certainly extended the horizon of possibilities in the sphere of work.

The caste system gave a distinctive, not to say a unique, character to work practices and norms in India. Not only was work elaborately differentiated and graded, but the gradation was sustained by ideas of purity and pollution that had deep roots in religious belief and practice. Elsewhere, the lowest types of work might be considered degrading or demeaning, in India they were treated as ritually defiling. Nowhere in the world was the idea of work as a source of defilement, even permanent and hereditary defilement, carried to such extremes as in India.

The stigma of pollution that was attached to such work as scavenging, tanning and flaying cast a shadow over many if not most kinds of manual and menial work. Oil-pressing, distilling, laundering, fishing and even ploughing the land were all considered as tainted in varying degrees.

Attitudes to work change, although the inertia of age-old habits of the mind should not be discounted. Economic change has loosened the association between caste and occupation, but its effect has been uneven rather than uniform. New occupations have emerged that are not directly associated with caste. This does not mean that they are not socially graded, but their gradation tends to be based on secular rather than ritual criteria.

Manual work is rated lower than non-manual work in all societies although the disparities tend to be larger in agrarian than in industrial societies. In India, manual workers prefer factory to farm work which they find unclean, tedious and exhausting. In areas of wet paddy cultivation, the lot of female agricultural labourers who have to do the bulk of the weeding and transplanting, often through heavy rain, is indeed very hard; it is no surprise that they prefer factory work to farm work.

Many factors have contributed to the moderation of the disparities between manual and non-manual work. In India the movement of people from the village to the city and from the farm to the office and the factory has been accompanied by what I have called the secularization of work. In the office and the factory, work continues to be differentiated and graded but the gradation is no longer governed by the ritual opposition of purity and pollution. It is far from my argument that the social ranking of occupations is disappearing or will disappear. The point simply is that the ranking acquires a new character when ritual criteria are displaced by secular ones.

Two important factors that are contributing to the secularization of work in our time are technological innovation and the spread of education. Good examples of the former may be found from the field of leatherwork. As is well known, it was considered highly polluting in the past and is still considered so in the rural areas where traditional processes continue to be used. Revolutionary changes in leather technology, some of them initiated in India, have largely removed the stigma of pollution from leatherwork in the modern factory. There are many areas in which technological change is obscuring the very distinction between manual and non-manual work.

Modern education introduces secular as against ritual criteria for distinctions of rank among occupations. Some occupations require high educational qualifications while others do not; the former enjoy higher esteem than the latter. Fifty years ago the gap between manual and non-manual workers was reinforced by the fact that the former were generally uneducated if not illiterate whereas the latter were educated. This is no longer true to the same extent. As manual workers become literate and educated, they are less likely to be overwhelmed by the thought that their work and their life itself is defiling. This will not amount to equal remuneration or equal esteem for all work; but it will be something.

11

Clash of Civilizations?

The publication by the American political scientist Samuel Huntington of a provocative article in the journal *Foreign Affairs* in 1993, followed by a book in 1996, gave wide currency to the thesis of the clash of civilizations. There was nothing very profound or original in the Huntington thesis, but its appearance was timely. The Soviet Union had collapsed, and real and imaginary fears about the extremism, fundamentalism and terrorism widespread in the Islamic world were beginning to be expressed by the American establishment and growing sections of the American public. The thesis was essentially about the clash between Western and Islamic values, but it was dressed, rather thinly at that, in the language of pervasive and ineluctable clashes between civilizations having different origins and different destinations.

My impression is that the thesis about the clash of civilizations has been coldly received in Europe. Roman Herzog, the president of the Federal Republic of Germany, spoke repeatedly against it, and a collection of his speeches with comments by some others was published in 1999 under the title *Preventing the Clash of Civilizations*. At a panel discussion in Gütersloh in Germany in 1997 at which I was present, the former prime minister of the Netherlands, Ruud

The Telegraph, 28 August 2003.

Lubbers, attacked the Huntington thesis strongly and, by Dutch standards, intemperately. Yet, Mr Huntington will have reason to be happy because there are strong echoes of his thesis in the current Bush doctrine relating to Iraq, Syria and other Islamic countries.

As every anthropologist knows, the concept of civilization is a difficult and ambiguous one, containing many snares and pitfalls. A few years ago, when Huntington gave a talk at the Delhi School of Economics, I put it to him that, as an anthropologist, I found the concept of civilization a difficult one, and asked him what his concept of it was. I was not the only one in the audience who concluded from his response that he had not given much thought to the idea. Nothing is easier than to talk about the clash of civilizations if you do not have a clear concept of civilization.

A civilization is at the very least a distinct configuration of ideas, beliefs and values. Undoubtedly, the configurations differ from one civilization to another. But these differences must be seen in their proper perspective. First, difference is not the same thing as incompatibility. Second, there are differences in ideas, beliefs and values not only between civilizations but also within each civilization; there is no civilization that does not embody a plurality of values, or is free from antinomies, by which I mean conflicts, oppositions and tensions among those values. And third, differences in ideas, beliefs and values must be distinguished from conflicts of interest; conflicts of interest are often particularly acute when groups compete to secure not different ends but the same ones.

The boundaries of civilizations, compared to those of nation states, are porous. Even in ancient and medieval times, human populations as well as ideas, beliefs and values flowed across the boundaries of civilizations. These flows have increased to such an extent in the last two hundred years that it would be appropriate to say that the modern world is marked by the interpenetration of civilizations. This does not mean that all civilizations are becoming alike. Differences among them continue to exist, but old forms of differentiation are displaced by new ones. The long-term trend of change in human society and culture is towards differentiation rather than homogenization.

To be sure there are ideologues in every civilization—in America, in the Islamic world, in India, and elsewhere—who would like to maintain closure of the boundaries of their own civilization. They argue that this is necessary in the interest of unity, harmony and balance: the intrusion of alien elements into a civilization, they say, is bound to upset its balance. But a civilization whose constituent elements are in perfect balance with each other is a dead civilization and not a living one. And a civilization that cannot accommodate a variety of traditions, seeking to maintain a jealous hold on only one single tradition, can hardly be called a civilization.

The tangled nature of the internal and external relations within and between civilizations is nicely brought out by the sharp differences in sentiment, perception and opinion between the French and the Germans on the one hand and the Americans on the other over the American invasion of Iraq. Obviously there are differences of political interest and strategy between the two sides, but each side is also accusing the other of deep and inherent moral flaws. It is not so uncommon to explain, or explain away, differences of political interest by reverting to ineluctable historical and cultural differences.

Books and articles are being written on anti-Europeanism in America and anti-Americanism in Europe. In this round of the culture wars it is the Americans who appear to have taken the initiative, but when it comes to culture, the French know how to give back as good as they get. A recent commentator has noted the 'paroxysms of sneering Europhobia in the US media'. The sneer is about the duplicity, hypocrisy and cowardice of the Europeans, and in particular the French, as against the manly virtues of the Americans: as the catch phrase has it, 'Americans are from Mars, Europeans are from Venus'. The French intellectual, who is nothing if not supercilious, might say that this is not a clash of civilizations, but a clash between civilization on one side of the Atlantic and its absence on the other.

The diatribes across the Atlantic have brought out certain interesting contrasts of cultural orientation as well as certain interesting reversals of contrast. The Americans are today riding the high horse of militarism whereas there is a genuine current of pacifism running through contemporary German society. But this contrast between American bellicosity and German pacifism is an almost exact reversal of the contrast between Germany and the United States one may have noted between, say, 1871 and 1941.

There have also been important shifts in patterns of inequality and attitudes to it on the two sides of the Atlantic. There is more equality and greater concern over inequality in France and Germany than in the United States today. This would have surprised Alexis de Tocqueville, the French aristocrat and theorist of democracy who had argued in the first half of the nineteenth century that the advance of equality was providential and that in that advance America would lead the way and Europe would follow. America still wants to lead the way, but not, it would appear, in the advance of equality.

It is not my argument that the divergence between Europe and America will continue indefinitely along the course it has taken now. There will be divergence and re-convergence, and then perhaps divergence again. All great civilizations recognize, acknowledge and accommodate the same basic and fundamental human values, but in very different combinations. Moreover, these combinations are in a perpetual process of change. That is why one has to approach with the utmost caution pronouncements on the clash of civilizations, whether between Islam and the West or between the United States and France.

12

Language and Civilization

A few years ago at a dinner in Tokyo hosted by the Japanese anthropologist Chie Nakane, I said somewhat light-heartedly to a Cambridge academic seated next to me that I did not think that the English were a particularly civilized people. My Cambridge friend took up the banter and challenged me to give him a definition of a civilized person. I accepted his challenge and said that for me a civilized person was simply a person who was at home in at least two different languages: having one language makes us human, being at home in more than one is what makes us civilized. Professor Nakane, who had been listening to the interchange with amusement, turned to me and said, 'Ah, that is a very Indian way of looking at civilization'. I was a little embarrassed because the Japanese are, if anything, even more inept than the English with languages other than their own.

The Japanese do many things very efficiently at which the Indians are rather inept, but the latter have an undeniable advantage over the former in the matter of languages. My Japanese students in Delhi often told me that while in Japan the students were very hard-working, in India they were more intelligent, but what they really meant was that the Indians were more articulate. It is a fact that an Indian can make a public speech at the drop of a hat whereas I am told that in Japan even the seasoned politician finds it hard to speak at a stretch for more than ten or fifteen minutes.

Indians owe their aptitude for language not to any superiority of racial or genetic endowment but to specific social and historical circumstances. They have for long lived in an environment that has tolerated and even encouraged diversity of social and cultural practices, including linguistic practices. The linguistic diversity of India is truly remarkable. In the past when a family, a kin group or a community moved from one region to another, its members acquired the language of their domicile without giving up the language of their ancestors. Bilingualism was widespread in both rural and urban areas, and even among the unlettered. In the village in Tanjore district where I did fieldwork in the 1960s, Telugu, Kannada and Marathi were spoken in some homes in addition to the Tamil that was spoken and understood by all.

To be sure, people do not learn new languages only because they are available for learning. Sometimes they are obliged to learn them from compulsions of one kind or another. But when the compulsion arises, a favourable disposition towards other languages goes a long way in meeting it. Although a favourable disposition towards other languages has been a part of the Indian cultural tradition, it faces threats from various quarters. The politics of language tends to create hostility to other languages in the name of attachment and loyalty to the mother tongue.

It is self-limiting to view other languages as threats to one's mother tongue, and a mistake to believe that human beings were created to express themselves or communicate with others in only one language. The English language has now come to occupy a pre-eminent place throughout the world. It is read, spoken and understood by more people than any language has ever been in human history. No doubt the spread of the English language in the nineteenth century was driven by the expansion of the British empire. Had some other nation extended its power instead of the British, some other language would have been the predominant language of the twentieth century. The fact is that the predominance of the English language has outlived the dissolution of the British empire, and there is little indication of a decline in its influence in the foreseeable future.

Learning English became very important for education and employment from the middle of the nineteenth century onwards. A new middle class began to emerge in the presidency centres at Calcutta, Bombay and Madras, and it gradually spread its influence throughout the country. Its members found places for themselves in a new occupational system, in the services of the government, and in law, medicine, teaching and other professions. The new middle class played a momentous part in shaping the economic, political and other institutions of contemporary India. Facility with the English language contributed much to the formation of all those modern institutions that we value today, although it did not come easily or without cost.

In some parts of the world the existing languages declined or died with the advance of dominant languages such as English, French and Spanish, but that did not happen in India. On the contrary, literary and journalistic writing in such languages as Bengali, Marathi and Tamil was enriched by the influence of English. The two great literary figures of nineteenth-century Bengal, Michael Madhusudan Dutt and Bankimchandra Chatterjee not only acquired effective command of the English language but also tried their hand at literary composition in that language. Their mastery of the English language and literature enabled them to experiment successfully with new literary forms in their own language.

Knowledge of the English language was sought because it gave access to gainful employment, but that was not its only attraction. It opened a window on to a new world. English books and periodicals brought to the doorstep of the Indian intelligentsia a whole new system of ideas, beliefs and values. Its social and political categories were different from the ones to which educated Indians had been accustomed for centuries. It is not as if reflective Indians had never thought about equality, liberty or progress, but they had thought about them in a language whose concepts and categories had become set in a particular mould. Their growing intimacy with a new language and idiom stimulated them to rethink their old categories and to explore new ones.

For all its troubles with alien rulers, an alien language and alien ways of life and thought, the Indian intelligentsia did not turn its back on the modern world. Modernization is today inescapable, but it is not a painless process, and it penalizes latecomers severely. Modernity does not presuppose a homogeneous world in which everybody does the same things, thinks the same thoughts and speaks the same language; on the contrary, it requires and encourages knowledge and appreciation of alternative ways of life. India is fortunate in having an educated middle class whose origins go back a hundred and fifty years in time. This middle class is now very large and differentiated. Despite regularly losing many of its ablest members to westward migration, it is replenished by increasing numbers of professional persons who are able to draw upon more than one intellectual tradition. The accumulated intellectual capital of this class is an asset whose value to society is not sufficiently appreciated and whose role is often thoughtlessly denigrated by the intelligentsia itself.

Differences of language divide people from each other,

but there is nothing inevitable about such divisions. Politics may be used either for deepening the divisions or for building bridges across them. The main point to bear in mind is that loyalty to language need not be singular since the same person may be attached to more than one language. This has been a common practice in India for a long time, and there is no reason why the practice cannot become more extensive in the future.

Their social tradition has given Indians an aptitude for languages that is sometimes better appreciated by others than by themselves. Max Gluckman, a British social anthropologist of South African origin once told me that the best English he had ever heard spoken was by an Indian called Srinivas Shastri. But whereas I could pronounce English names easily and clearly, Professor Gluckman had the greatest difficulty in pronouncing the name of the silver-tongued orator. That of course confirmed the point he was making, namely, that the British were hopeless when it came to languages other than their own.

13

Speaking and Writing

Indians are much more at ease with the spoken than with the written word. They speak eloquently and with evident pleasure, but their writing is often hasty and careless. It is of course true that vast numbers of Indians lack the capacity to use the written word altogether. But there are many others who do have that capacity, and my purpose here is to draw attention to the ways in which they use and misuse it. The most common way of misusing it is to write at excessive and unnecessary length.

I am of course aware that there are first-rate poets, playwrights and novelists in several Indian languages who write clearly and elegantly, and even economically. But I am not concerned here with individual talent. My concern is with attitudes to writing common among those who have to use the written word in the course of their ordinary work, such as scholars, journalists, civil servants and even judges. Here there is remarkable laxity not only in the way things get written but also in allowing them to get into print. Reading and writing were known in India well before they were known in the West, yet our basic attitudes are those of an oral rather than a written culture.

Indians excel with the spoken word. Anyone who belongs

The Telegraph, 6 April 2005.

to that large and ill-defined category known as public intellectuals in India can speak at any length and on almost any subject. Not only that: he can speak without reference to any notes and often without much application of the mind. Western academics are often struck by the fact that their Indian counterparts can speak fluently and effortlessly, if not always faultlessly, without consulting notes.

I may illustrate the contrast from my experience of two lectures that I gave at two premier universities each of which was chaired by the vice-chancellor of the university concerned. The first lecture was at the University of Cambridge where the vice-chancellor was a distinguished medical scientist. He introduced me briefly and, after I had concluded, also thanked me briefly. As we were walking out, he told me that he had greatly enjoyed my lecture. When I remonstrated that he was merely being polite, he quietly took out the notes he had made during the lecture which ran into three pages: he had come to the lecture to listen rather than to speak.

At the other lecture in the Indian university, the vice-chancellor arrived thirty-five minutes late while the speaker and the audience waited. Having arrived late, he embarked on a lengthy and eloquent speech on the challenges facing the country and the need for teachers and students to rise up to them. By the time he sat down and I began my lecture on whose preparation I had spent more than a month, it became evident that he and most of the audience had lost interest in it. As to taking notes, here no self-respecting vice-chancellor takes notes at a lecture given by a mere professor.

Indian academics like to say that the defects of academic prose in India are due to the use of a foreign language. This is only a small part of the story. The more important part is the lack of patience and care in the writing. If Indians find it a struggle to write in English, why do they write at such immoderate length? The problem is not lack of facility with the language but lack of measure and discipline which escapes notice more easily in speech than in writing. The same lack of measure and discipline, and the same excessive length may be found in our judicial as in our academic prose. Commenting on the inordinate length of our Supreme Court judgements, Mr Nani Palkhiwala had once observed that they give clear evidence of the Indian preoccupation with eternity and infinity.

Indians of standing do not like being interrupted while they are talking, but they do not seem to mind when what they have written is revised or even rewritten. Mr Sham Lal, under whose tutelage I began writing for the newspapers, would tell me about his tribulations with academic writers. He took pains to offer the columns of the editorial pages of the *Times of India* to distinguished academics. But what they sent him was often carelessly and badly written. When he revised and sometimes rewrote their pieces, they rarely objected; perhaps they did not notice.

A senior colleague once sent me an advance copy of a book review. Since the author of the book had been his teacher as well as mine, he wanted to make sure that the review would not cause offence. What struck me about the review was not that it was critical but that it was twenty-seven pages in length. When I pointed out that it was far too long to fit into the Sunday newspaper for which it was written, he agreed and added genially that the editors would reduce it to the required length. It is not simply that I knew that the review was far too long; he also knew it.

A great English historian wrote that reading and writing are solitary pursuits while talking is a way of being gregarious. The Indian is gregarious by nature. He finds it hard to be solitary unless he is a sannyasi or a poet. From childhood he grows up in the company of others: relatives of many different kinds, friends and neighbours. He is discouraged from being by himself, and made to believe that being by oneself is a way of being selfish and arrogant. In adult life, if he achieves any standing at all, he is continuously surrounded by others. As he grows in stature, his visitors grow in number and variety.

During my long period of service in the University of Delhi I often wondered how vice-chancellors, deans and principals ever found time to think, since they were constantly surrounded by people. Though my experience of professional life in the West is limited, it is difficult not to notice the contrast. It is not that professionals there do not have to spend time in meetings or do not enjoy committee work, but they are also mindful of the time they need to be by themselves. Successful Indian academics complain endlessly of the time they have to spend on meetings and committees, but their complaints need not be taken seriously. They relish nothing more than being surrounded by people before whom they can hold forth; what they cannot bear is being by themselves.

Being able to write clearly and well is not just a matter of intelligence or even facility with language. Above all, it requires patience and care, and emotional investment of a certain kind. Where so much is invested in being gregarious, the concentration of effort required for serious writing naturally suffers. Obviously, there are individuals who are masters of both the spoken and the written word. Such individuals are outstanding, and are therefore not confined by their circumstances but are able to rise above them. That apart, there appear to be marked differences of general orientation between cultures. Some cultures tolerate careless, disjointed and vacuous writing while others discourage it.

14

Editorial Vandalism

Cultural anthropologists give a special place in their work to the interpretation of apparently irrational behaviour. The really ingenious ones among them try to persuade their readers that such practices as cannibalism, head-hunting and the burning of widows have an inner logic in whose light they appear intelligible, meaningful and even reasonable. My imagination does not extend that far. The puzzle that I would like to share with my readers is about the conduct of editors in their relations with the authors whose works they undertake to prepare for publication.

As an author of books and articles in journals, magazines and newspapers, I have been a victim of editorial caprice for more than three decades. Editors, assistant editors and sub-editors work on manuscripts and transform them into printed matter that the author often finds puzzling, and at times incomprehensible. The editor on the other hand feels that the chopping, and pruning and embellishing that he does is in the common interest of both the reader and the author. Personally speaking, I fear the embellishment more than the chopping and pruning.

Not all editors are equally heavy handed. Some are in fact patient and solicitous, but the majority of them allow their

The Telegraph, 8 June 2003.

zeal for improving the copy in hand to overtake their better judgement. I am not suggesting that authorial prose is never in need of improvement. In fact, much of the writing that is submitted for publication is slipshod, repetitive and prolix. I know reputed academic authors who disdain to cross the 't's and dot the 'i's in what they write because they believe that there are copy editors who are paid to do the job; some write with abandon and at breakneck speed, and then have little time left to read what they have written. However, this article is about editorial vandalism and not about authorial irresponsibility which is a separate subject.

There are major differences between the editing of newspaper articles and of scholarly books. My tales of woe relate mainly to the latter, but I must first say a few words about the former. Newspaper editors have far less time than the editors of scholarly books to tinker with the matter they have to send to press. In my experience, they tend to go for the title rather than the text. When they feel well disposed towards an author, they accept more or less whatever he sends, checking for length—and frequency of submission—but not always giving attention to facts or arguments. Where they like to have their way is in the invention of a new title. I suppose they believe that no matter what the article says, the title must be catchy. Not infrequently, there is no obvious connection between the title and the text, and title and text sometimes contradict each other.

Editing a book or even a paper for a scholarly journal is a somewhat different matter. It is generally done not by a single person but by a hierarchy of persons, starting with the commissioning editor and ending with the copy editor; even the proof-reader sometimes takes a hand at improving the author's language. The unwary author might feel that his battle is over when he has got past the commissioning editor or his immediate subordinate, but his real trouble often begins with the copy editor. I have passed through the hands of many copy editors, including both seasoned professionals and young graduates fresh from the university.

Copy-editing is not about the general structure or the overall length of the work. It is about making the work compact, readable and, as far as possible, free from errors and inconsistencies of language. The reason that copy editors most commonly give for making drastic changes is that the copy they receive is full of mistakes. One has to make a distinction between a work that contains mistakes and one that lacks style. Allowing a manuscript to go to the printers without removing the mistakes in it would be irresponsible. But improving or embellishing an author's style is a different matter altogether. The problem is that the editor with even a good command of the language may be only vaguely familiar with the discipline the author professes. Then in his effort to embellish the author's prose, the editor alters his meaning without always realizing what he has done.

Editorial vandalism is not a matter of correcting mistakes, or even of chopping and pruning; it is the expression of an urge to improve and embellish the author's language without understanding, or even seriously attempting to understand, what the author wishes to say. My impression is that it takes certain distinctive forms in English-language editing in India and that it has become more widespread in recent times.

Part of the problem arises from the peculiar attitude to the English language among members of the Indian middle class. Command over English, which is very unevenly spread in that class, is not only an important intellectual resource, it is also an important marker of social status. Correcting and improving another person's English is to establish not only one's intellectual but also one's social superiority over him.

There is no more effective way of putting an author in his place than to show up his deficiency in English. As someone who has published in both Britain and India, I have found that British copy editors are far less anxious to improve and embellish an author's English than are their Indian counterparts.

The most important practical reason why copy editors make alterations in manuscripts is that they are paid to do so. Here a change has come about in the organization of work in publishing houses, particularly the larger ones. Copy-editing has become a specialized job and it tends to be outsourced, that is assigned to freelancers. I am told that publishing houses find this more economical, particularly when the copy editor is young and unseasoned, and does not have to be paid at a high rate.

In the past, copy-editing was mainly in-house work, and even senior editors did not disdain to do it. My own work was copy-edited at Oxford University Press by Ravi Dayal, one of the finest editors in the country, and he continued to do the work even after he became general manager, something that would be considered a monstrous waste of resources today. It is true that he took a perverse pleasure in pointing out all my mistakes and infelicities, but he also taught me many things for which I still remain grateful.

Things have now changed. Copy-editing is outsourced to freelancers who are paid by the page for the work they do. I am told that the rates are not very high and not attractive enough to induce talented persons to view it as a long-term commitment. When a copy editor is paid by the page, it is natural for him to feel, particularly if he is young and inexperienced, that he should not leave too many pages unmarked. He must give some evidence that he has applied himself to his task, and what better evidence can there be than blue and red pencil marks across the manuscript?

III
Village, Caste and Family

Village, caste and family have been the key institutions of Indian society from ancient to modern times. Many changes have taken place in them in the last hundred years but their continuing importance in contemporary India cannot be gainsaid.

The Indian village has been a subject of serious study as well as much myth-making. The nationalist movement promoted the myth of the Indian village as a peaceful, harmonious and self-sufficient community. The reality as revealed by studies in different parts of the country by sociologists and social anthropologists is very different. This is partly because the village today is not what it was a hundred or a hundred and fifty years ago. But even then it was permeated by division and hierarchy.

Caste too has been changing continuously since the end of the nineteenth century. While its ritual aspects, based on ideas of purity and pollution, have undergone continuous decline, democratic politics has given caste a new lease of life. All political parties have used the loyalties of caste as a basis for mobilizing electoral support, and caste identities continue to be very strong. There is much continuity in Indian society between caste and kinship and, while inter-caste marriages are definitely on the increase, caste in the extended sense continues to be an important factor in matrimonial choice among most Indians in most parts of the country.

15

Village Republics

The Indian intelligentsia has somewhat mixed attitudes towards the Indian village. While educated Indians are inclined to think or at least speak well of the village, they do not show much inclination for the company of villagers. The late Professor M.N. Srinivas, who sent me out to live in a Tanjore village and to do fieldwork there, often pointed to this paradoxical feature of Indian life. He himself had started his fieldwork in a Mysore village by living in a cowshed to which he had been consigned by the peasant elders who felt that, being a Brahmin, he would be defiled by living in their homes whereas in the cowshed his purity would remain intact. Srinivas wanted me to live in the village for a whole year so that I could learn from observation and experience that the idea of the harmonious village community was a myth.

This was a period of enthusiasm for Panchayati Raj and Community Development. Experts came from far and wide to give advice on these subjects. Srinivas heaped scorn on their research because he had found out that they went to the village by car and returned to their hotels by sundown. He believed that one could never learn about a village unless one ate and slept there, continuously for days, weeks and months at a time. I did all those things but from the modest comfort of a brick-and-tile house in the *agraharam*.

The enthusiasm for Panchayati Raj, Community Development, and what may be described as 'villageism' declined after the 1960s, but it did not die out. It has been revived with the 73rd Constitutional Amendment and the creation of a new type of panchayat in its wake. Many have come to believe that it is through these reconstituted panchayats that women, Harijans and other disadvantaged sections of society will come to take their rightful places in village India, if not in India as a whole.

Village councils in which women and Harijans have a central place will be a genuine institutional innovation and not a return to the institutions of the pre-colonial village. This must not be lost sight of in the enthusiasm for the village republics that are expected to give a new lease of life to democracy in India. It is not quite clear how far those who initiated the 73rd Constitutional Amendment were aware of the break they were seeking to introduce into India's rural society. They appear to have genuinely believed that some kind of village democracy had been the norm in the past.

There is nothing unusual or novel in the city-bred person's belief in the regenerative powers of the village. In a set of lectures delivered at Aligarh thirty years ago, the historian Niharranjan Ray drew attention to the urban Indian's perennial nostalgia for the village. This nostalgia, he said, had been expressed since the nineteenth century in literary form in fiction and poetry and in political form in the slogan of 'back to the villages'. He observed, 'The curious aspect of the whole thing is that with but few exceptions these writers and poets and these nationalist leaders were all city-dwellers, not villagers themselves, nor were they ever thinking of trekking back to the villages to live there.'

The two most outstanding Indians of the period before independence, Rabindranath Tagore and Mahatma Gandhi were both actively interested in the village and in its reconstruction. Yet, as Ray pointed out, Rabindranath was born and brought up in the city of Calcutta. Gandhi's family too was town based rather than village based. Neither of them had experienced at first hand the harsh realities of village life in either childhood or adolescence. They turned to the village in adult life after they had formed a view of the world in which the village stood for the core values of Indian civilization.

Detailed and intensive research by sociologists, social anthropologists and others on the Indian village began almost immediately after independence. Indeed, the fifties and sixties of the last century may be described as the great age of village studies. These studies were made by both Indian and foreign scholars and there was genuine collaboration between them. Sociological research on the Indian village has lost some of its momentum, but it continues, and we now have re-studies of villages first studied in the 1950s and 1960s. It will be safe to say that the research on the Indian village is fuller and deeper than on the village anywhere else in the world. Yet, legislators, policy makers and activists appear to have paid very little heed to the results of this research.

The picture that we get of the Indian village from the researches conducted by sociologists and social anthropologists is very different from the village of the nationalist or literary imagination. The picture is by no means uniform, but division and hierarchy figure prominently almost everywhere. There is the division and hierarchy due to caste, but there are also deep divisions arising from inequalities in the ownership, control and use of land; and men and women have different and unequal positions everywhere, including tribal villages which are relatively less hierarchical. Changes are no doubt taking place in the villages, but those changes have not led to the elimination of either division or inequality.

Village councils, no matter how they are reconstituted, will have to operate in a matrix pervaded by social divisions and social inequalities. Those divisions and inequalities cannot be conjured out of existence by an Act of Parliament, no matter how progressive, or by the zeal of social activists, no matter how deeply committed. If the Indian intelligentsia has a remarkable capacity for anything, it is the capacity for wishful thinking. It is this wishful thinking that leads them to believe that all will again be well with Indian democracy, once women and other disadvantaged members of society are made *sarpanches* throughout the land.

As against the benign views of the Indian village taken by Tagore and Gandhi, Dr Ambedkar spoke about it bluntly and unsentimentally. He articulated a kind of experience that neither Tagore nor Gandhi could have possibly had in their formative years. He told the Constituent Assembly, 'I hold that these village republics have been the ruination of India,' and went on to ask, 'What is the village but a sink of localism, a den of ignorance, narrow-mindedness and communalism?' He wondered how those who were so strongly opposed to communalism, casteism and factionalism in the nation could be so blind to their presence in the village.

It is now more than fifty years since Dr Ambedkar issued his warning in the Constituent Assembly against idealizing the village community. Several institutional innovations have been attempted in the intervening years to make democracy more effective and meaningful, and several more will be attempted in the years to come. It will be imprudent to expect each successive innovation to accomplish what all previous ones have failed to do. It will be no less imprudent to write off every fresh experiment on the ground that where earlier ones have failed, later ones can never succeed. At the same time, it must not be forgotten that social and political experiments have unintended consequences, and there must be some assessment, in the light of past experience, not only of their anticipated benefits but also of their anticipated costs.

Social research conducted over a long period of time by independent institutions is invaluable in assessing long-term trends of change. Such research must be insulated not only from bureaucratic interference but also from social advocacy. We do not as yet have reliable accounts, based on cumulative research, of how the new panchayats are working. Reports based on short-term and ad hoc studies sponsored by the advocates of the system cannot be a substitute for independent research. Social research and social advocacy need not be enemies of each other, but very often they are.

16

Caste and Colonial Rule

Is there a secular trend of decline in the strength of caste in Indian society? My assessment is that there is, although one cannot be categorical because there are many counter-currents that act against the main current. Further, I believe that the trend of change towards the weakening of caste began during British rule around the middle of the nineteenth century and has continued, with many ups and downs, till the present. This view is at odds with the current enthusiasm for identity politics in which signs of the growing importance of caste are seen as indications of a progressive movement towards the attainment of social justice.

In the early years of independence, forward-looking Indians had their minds on development and modernization; and when they thought of caste, they thought of it as an obstacle to them. Liberal and radical intellectuals alike believed that caste belonged to India's past, not its future.

Marxists were particularly scornful of those who undertook to study and write about caste. They believed that it was a fit subject for bourgeois sociologists but not for those concerned with the real contradictions in society. When I brought up the subject in a conversation with E.M.S. Namboodiripad in the mid-1970s, he put me down genially and without malice

---

The Hindu, 4 March 2002.

by saying that, like most Indian anthropologists, I was obsessed with caste because of our common enslavement to American social science. Marxists then took a negative view of caste because they believed that caste consciousness was an obstacle to class formation.

Caste consciousness may well be an obstacle to class formation, but we cannot for that or any other reason wish it out of existence. Caste continued to receive the attention of sociologists and social anthropologists in the 1950s and 1960s, and they were joined by small numbers of political scientists and others. It was M.N. Srinivas who more than any other scholar pointed to the continuing, and in some respects increasing, importance of caste. When in 1957 he said in his presidential address at the Indian Science Congress that caste was acquiring a new lease of life through electoral politics, his view was widely criticized. Later events confounded the critics and showed that Srinivas had been substantially right.

Without taking anything away from Srinivas's foresight, it must be pointed out that in making his case about the resurgence of caste in independent India, he took all his examples from the field of politics. If we focus attention on the political process alone, we are likely to conclude that caste has grown stronger and not weaker since the time of the Emergency. Caste is now used more extensively and more openly for the mobilization of political support than it was ever before.

If our objective is to assess long-term trends of change in caste, it will be a mistake to concentrate solely on politics, and that too on electoral politics. A serious weakness in the scholarly writing on caste in the last twenty-five years and particularly since the time of the Mandal agitations has been the neglect of all aspects of caste other than the political. The association between caste and occupation has weakened, slowly but steadily. While restrictions on marriage are still observed, the rules of endogamy are enforced far less stringently than before. As to the ritual practices of purity and pollution, which many regarded as the very cement of caste, all the evidence shows that they are clearly and decisively in retreat.

The changes that have been taking place in caste since independence began at least a hundred years before independence, under colonial rule. If the Constitution of India is a landmark in the history of caste, an earlier though less conspicuous landmark is the Removal of Caste Disabilities Act of 1850. Until then the life of a Hindu was so deeply embedded in his caste that expulsion from it virtually amounted to civil death.

Colonial administrators, like administrators everywhere, were inclined to take more than their due share of credit for bringing about beneficent changes in the country they administered. They exaggerated the rigidity and oppressiveness of the traditional social order and their own role in establishing liberal ideas and institutions in India. Many of their acts did indeed lead to the weakening of caste, but some also led to its strengthening. On balance, however, the long-term consequence of colonial rule was the weakening rather than the strengthening of caste, whatever may have been the intentions with which individual administrators acted.

Many British administrators took an obsessive interest in caste, and it is obvious that their interest was not based only on natural or benign curiosity. Some of it arose from the desire to show how backward Indian society was and how uncongenial it was for democracy. But we must not judge the British too harshly for their strictures on Indian society, for Dr Ambedkar had himself said in the Constituent Assembly that 'democracy in India is only a top-dressing on an Indian soil that is essentially undemocratic'.

Having learnt about the divisive possibilities inherent in caste, the British were not slow to use those possibilities for their own political and administrative ends. Here they were only showing the way to the rulers of independent India who have outclassed their British predecessors in using the loyalties of caste for mobilizing political support, particularly after 1977. And if our present leaders say that they are using caste only in the interest of social justice, the British too believed or at least said that their main interest was to ensure fair treatment, in a caste-divided society, for the minorities, the depressed classes and the backward communities.

Colonial administrators wrote a great deal about caste, and much of what they wrote was biased as is indeed the case with official writing anywhere. For a hundred years they set about identifying, enumerating, describing, classifying and ranking the different castes and communities in the subcontinent. The decennial censuses played some part in bringing to public attention the division and ranking of castes. It is for this reason that it was decided not to enumerate castes in the censuses after the new government took office on the attainment of independence. But while the censuses and ethnographic reports may have created a new sense of rivalry among castes, the institution of caste itself had deep roots in the Indian soil.

For all its fascination for the enumeration and classification of castes—inherited to some extent by our present census takers and official ethnographers—colonial rule loosened the soil in which caste had been rooted for centuries. It introduced new economic forces and a new legal and social philosophy. It established a new educational system and a new occupational system based on principles antithetical to the hierarchical principles of caste. It is true that the creation of new institutions was not a painless process; but those institutions helped to carry India forward into the modern world.

It has now become increasingly common to represent colonial rule as the source and origin of every economic, political and social malady present in contemporary India. Some smart American historians have even floated the idea that caste as we know it today is basically a creation of colonial rule, and that idea has naturally found many subscribers among Indians. There is no need now to whitewash colonial rule; but there is no need either to deny the advances in Indian society that started under it. Today historians of the left seem to vie with those of the right in depicting colonial rule in the darkest of colours. This is completely contrary to the historical perspective of Marx who took the view, essentially correct in my judgement, that on balance colonial rule was a progressive force in nineteenth-century India. We cannot get the history of independent India right if we are so wrong in our reading of what happened in the hundred years before independence.

17

Race and Caste

As a student of anthropology in Calcutta in the 1950s, I was recommended a book written by the well-known physical anthropologist M.F. Ashley Montagu, some of whose other works we also had to study. The book to which I now refer was entitled *Man's Most Dangerous Myth: The Fallacy of Race*. Ashley Montagu had overstated his case somewhat, but the basic point he was making, that the widely used concept of race was politically pernicious and scientifically anomalous, had come to be generally accepted among anthropologists by the middle of the twentieth century.

Some anthropologists attended to the political mischief caused by the idea of race while others exposed its scientific ambiguities. The most notable among the latter was Franz Boas, widely regarded as the father of American anthropology. In his book, *Race, Language and Culture*, he established conclusively with a wealth of empirical material the distinction between race, which is a biological category with physical markers, and social groupings based on language, religion, nationality, style of life or status. Boas's conclusion may be regarded as the settled opinion on the subject among professional anthropologists the world over.

Race, Language and Culture, published in 1940, was the

The Hindu, 10 March 2001.

culmination of systematic and painstaking research by two or three generations of anthropologists. In the nineteenth century, when anthropology was still largely an amateur pursuit, the concept of race was widely and loosely used to cover virtually every kind of social grouping. One read about the Aryan race, the Semitic race and the Irish race. The influential French writer Count Gobineau even proposed that the different classes in France were composed of different races. In fact, race and class were linked together in Europe even before attempts were made to link race and caste in India. Pseudo-scientific theories of race abounded in the late nineteenth- and early twentieth-century Europe and America. They made no small contribution to Hitler's disastrous racial policies in Germany. Although the English, the French and the Americans adopted a self-consciously virtuous attitude after 1945, they too produced an abundance of pseudo-scientific theories of race before the Second World War.

At about the same period of time, the Indian Civil Service counted a fair number of amateur anthropologists in its ranks. Some of them have left behind valuable accounts of the tribes and castes of India. Others took an interest in race that at times amounted to an obsession. The obsessive ones found evidence of racial difference wherever they looked. Their main confusion was between race and language, and they wrote freely about the 'Aryan race' and the 'Dravidian race'. Some treated the Hindus and Muslims as belonging to different races, and others expressed similar views about the upper and the lower castes. These views, based on a confusion of categories, are now regarded as worthless from the scientific point of view.

It is not as if there was no serious scientific effort by the ICS anthropologists to study the racial composition of the Indian population. Several of them attended to the problem with patience and care, combining the study of physical features with that of social customs. The most notable was Sir Herbert Risley who produced a comprehensive classification of the races of India into seven types. But the principal 'racial types' in his classification—Aryan, Dravidian, Aryo-Dravidian and Mongolo-Dravidian—were linguistic or regional categories in disguise and not racial categories at all. The subsequent classification by B.S. Guha, made in connection with the census of 1931, was less ambitious, for it did not speak of 'racial types' but only of 'racial elements' in the population of the country.

By the mid-1950s when I was a student of anthropology, most anthropologists had lost interest in the racial classification of the Indian population. Although there were many different racial elements in it, it was difficult, if not impossible, to sort them out into distinct racial groups. In the 1970s, I took some interest on behalf of the Oxford University Press to update Guha's work on racial elements. I approached a number of physical anthropologists, but they either declined or said that they would do it but failed to deliver. I am now convinced that identifying the races in the population of India will be an exercise in futility.

Despite all the hard work done by anthropologists from Boas onward, the idea of race dies hard in the popular imagination. That is understandable. What is neither understandable nor excusable is the attempt by the United Nations on the eve of the Durban Conference in August 2001 to revive and expand the idea of race, ostensibly to combat the many forms of social and political discrimination prevalent in the world. It is sad but true that many forms of invidious discrimination do prevail in the contemporary world. But to assimilate or even relate them all to 'racial discrimination' will be an act of political and moral irresponsibility.

Not content with condemning racism and racial

discrimination, the UN now wants to take on 'racism, racial discrimination, xenophobia and related intolerance'. It has in its wisdom decided to expand the meaning of racial discrimination to accommodate exclusion or preference 'based on race, colour, descent, or national or ethnic origin'. In doing so it is bound to give a new lease of life to the old and discredited notion of race current a hundred years ago. By flying in the face of the distinctions between race, language and culture, it is seeking to undo the conclusions reached by the researches of several generations of anthropologists.

Interested parties within and outside the United Nations would like to bring caste discrimination in general and the practice of untouchability in particular within the purview of racial discrimination. The practice of untouchability is indeed reprehensible and must be condemned by one and all; but that does not mean that we should now begin to regard it as a form of racial discrimination. The Scheduled Castes taken together are no more a race than are the Brahmins taken together. Every social group cannot be regarded as a race simply because we want to protect it against prejudice and discrimination.

In the past some groups claimed superior rights on the ground that they belonged to the Aryan race or the Teutonic race. The anthropologists rejected such claims on two grounds: first, on the ground that within the same human species no race is superior to any other; but also on the ground that there is no such thing as an Aryan race or a Teutonic race. We cannot throw out the concept of race by the front door when it is misused for asserting social superiority and bring it in again through the back door to misuse it in the cause of the oppressed. The metaphor of race is a dangerous weapon whether it is used for asserting white supremacy or for making demands on behalf of disadvantaged groups.

If discrimination against disadvantaged castes can be defined as a form of racial discrimination, there is no reason why discrimination, real or alleged, against religious or linguistic minorities cannot be phrased in exactly the same terms. The Muslims and other religious minorities will claim that they too, and not just backward castes, are victims of racial discrimination. The initiative taken by the United Nations is bound to encourage precisely that kind of claim.

The UN initiative will open up a Pandora's box of allegations of racial discrimination throughout the world. The latitudinarian attitude of the UN will encourage religious and other 'ethnic' minorities to make allegations of racial discrimination not only in India, but everywhere. The Catholics in Northern Ireland can claim that they too are victims of racial discrimination. The French Canadians, whose grievances are real enough, can also make the same claim. One can multiply examples from every corner of the world. By treating caste discrimination as a form of racial discrimination and, by implication, caste as a form of race, the United Nations is turning its back on established scientific opinion. One can only guess under what kind of pressure it is doing so. Treating caste as a form of race is politically mischievous; what is worse, it is scientifically nonsensical.

18

Inter-caste Marriage

Is caste growing stronger or weaker in contemporary India? This question is not easy to answer because the evidence does not all point in the same direction. The evidence from politics points in one direction and the evidence from marriage in another. Fifty years ago, educated Indians who looked to the future took it for granted that caste would decline steadily with the advance of democracy and development. There is now no longer the same optimism about either development or democracy. More and more Indians are becoming inured to the presence of caste in politics as they have become inured to the presence of corruption in it.

When M.N. Srinivas stated in a presidential address at the Science Congress in 1957 that caste was acquiring a new lease of life in independent India, many felt that his remarks were exaggerated if not outrageous. Yet the course of electoral politics has on the whole vindicated Srinivas and confounded his critics. At the same time, all the evidence that he provided in support of his argument came from the field of politics, and hardly any from other fields of social life. Many commentators have since noted the enlarged role of caste in politics; and some have even welcomed it as an expression of subaltern consciousness.

The Telegraph, 17 October 2002.

If we look at the literature on caste in the period before independence, we will find very little discussion in it of caste and politics. Much more attention was paid to caste and occupation, caste and ritual, and caste and marriage. In all these areas, the hold of caste is being weakened, clearly and visibly in some cases and slowly and imperceptibly in others. The disproportionate media attention given to politics creates the misleading impression that caste as a whole is becoming stronger.

The decline in the association between caste and occupation has been noted by many and over a long stretch of time. N.K. Bose showed through the analysis of census and other data how new economic forces were leading people to give up their traditional occupations to enter new 'caste-free' ones. This of course does not mean that occupations are no longer ranked, or even that there is no correlation between occupational rank and caste rank; but that correlation is now weaker than in the past.

Even while he was writing about the increasing role of caste in politics, Srinivas was pointing to a secular decline in attitudes and practices relating to purity and pollution. For many of those who wrote on the subject a hundred years ago, the rules of caste were mainly the rules of ritual. These rules, relating to food transactions, bodily contact and residential segregation, were many and diverse, and they contributed substantially to the perpetuation of division and hierarchy in the caste system. They are now incontestably in decline, and even the promoters of Hindutva would hesitate to call for their reinforcement.

Considerations of purity and pollution were closely tied to restrictions relating to marriage. Those restrictions have not been relaxed to nearly the same extent as the ones on the sharing and exchange of food and water. Many would say that the real acid test of the strength of caste lies in the durability of marriage restrictions. For it is through them that caste identities are maintained and reproduced. So long as they survive, caste will survive, with or without the benefit of electoral politics.

Restrictions on marriage were a feature of all hierarchical societies, but the ones associated with caste were exceptionally elaborate and stringent. They were specified in the classical laws of ancient and medieval India, and ethnographers recorded the same kinds of restrictions among the people they observed in the late nineteenth and the early twentieth centuries. Until recent times, their violation could lead to expulsion from caste which, at least among upper-caste Hindus, amounted to civil death.

Although inter-caste marriages are now taking place, there is little reliable or systematic data as to their frequency. Most marriages, even in the urban middle classes, are still arranged by parents and elders, and here caste is an important consideration. The matrimonial columns of the Sunday papers show that not many Indians are prepared to take chances with caste while seeking a bride or a groom. But there is evidence of some relaxation even in these advertisements. And with increasing education and employment among women and their increasing age at marriage, more and more individuals are marrying on their own, without recourse to traditional matchmakers or newspaper advertisements.

A study of inter-caste marriage by C.T. Kannan, published in 1963, showed that changes had already begun to take place. Kannan's sample was relatively small, but his evidence was clear. He wrote, 'Just twenty-five years ago (i.e. before World War II) the instances of inter-caste marriages were very few; and those individuals who dared to marry outside the caste had to undergo great hardships. Today the situation is altogether different.' Kannan pointed not only to the increased frequency of inter-caste marriages but also to their increased social acceptance. These changes are incremental rather than radical, but there can be little doubt about their direction.

No matter how strong the inertia of practice may be, the traditional rules of marriage are changing, and the sanctions behind them weakening. In the past one had to take into account not only the caste but also the sub-caste, and sometimes even the sub-sub-caste in arranging a marriage. Today marriages between sub-castes of the same caste are common, and a marriage may even be arranged between persons belonging to different but adjacent castes. This enlargement of choice in the arrangement of marriage does not receive media attention, but it is important.

In the past, marriages were regulated not only by the rule of endogamy but also by the rule of hypergamy. The first rule required a person to marry within his or her own caste or sub-caste. The second rule, known as *anuloma*, allowed a man to marry a woman from a caste or sub-caste inferior to his own, whereas *pratiloma*, or the union of a woman with a man inferior to her in caste rank, was strictly forbidden. The very ideas of anuloma and pratiloma are now becoming obsolete among educated urban Indians. Among them where people accept an inter-caste marriage, they are not inclined to ask whether it is of the anuloma kind which was approved under specific conditions or of the pratiloma kind which was condemned without exception.

A consideration of inter-caste marriages shows that the sanctions of caste have declined steadily in the last fifty years. What keeps the frequency of such marriages low are the sanctions of the family in the restricted or extended sense rather than of the caste or even the sub-caste as a community.

Inter-caste marriages will continue to increase, but not very dramatically. This is not because the community's resistance to such marriages is holding its strength, but because when it comes to family and marriage, middle-class Indians are reluctant to take even small risks.

19

The Changing Indian Family

What is it that Indians value most, something that they regard as an end in itself and for whose well-being they are prepared to sacrifice their personal needs and interests? This is a difficult question to answer at a time when old social arrangements such as those based on caste are breaking down, and new ones based on individual ability and achievement have at best a precarious foothold. At such a time of transition, cynicism becomes widespread, and many if not most middle-class Indians say that the only thing about which people care today is making money and getting ahead in the world without any regard for principles or values.

Such a cynical view does not appear wholly convincing even to those who put it forward. The pursuit of individual self-interest has its limits. The individual cares not only for himself but also for others, if not their well-being, then at least their praise, their esteem and their loyalty. Especially in India, the individual is emotionally dependent to an unusual degree on others, on their assurance, goodwill and support. This dependence is a social fact to the extent that it has an institutional focus, and, all things considered, it is in the family that it has today its clearest institutional focus.

In the past, a significant focus of attachment was provided

The Telegraph, 14 June 1997.

by caste which was in a sense the pre-eminent social institution, especially for the Hindus. The order of varna was for centuries the moral order of society, but this is no longer the case, and it is significant that Bengalis no longer speak or write of caste as varna but as jati, signalling a shift in its meaning and significance. To be sure, caste maintains a strong grip over politics in many parts of the country, but caste today is largely a matter of politics and hardly a matter of morality. The very people who make use of it in politics rarely feel that they owe very much to it. This is quite different from how their ancestors felt towards their caste or how they themselves feel towards their family.

There is of course religion whose pervasive hold over Indians in every walk of life is beyond dispute. But religion acts on the individual in many institutional spheres, ranging from the domestic to the political. Indeed, the increasingly aggressive intrusion of religion into the political sphere has become a source of anxiety to many. But there are other spheres of society in which religion has an important and a legitimate place. Pre-eminent among these is the family, for among Hindus and indeed most Indians, the most significant religious observances are those centring around the crucial events of birth, marriage and death.

To say that the family continues to be an institution of great importance in contemporary India is not to suggest that it is not undergoing changes. These changes are most conspicuous among the urban middle classes, but they extend to other sectors of society as well. At the same time, there are wide misconceptions about what the Indian family was like in the past and what it is likely to become in the future. Many educated persons believe that Indians in the past generally lived in large extended households which are now being rapidly replaced, at least in the cities, by nuclear families of the Western type. Both conceptions are largely mistaken.

First, it is important to distinguish between the family which is a kin group of variable scope and the household which is a residential unit. Careful demographic analysis, notably by the sociologist A.M. Shah, has revealed that the average size of the household has undergone hardly any change in the last hundred and fifty years. Such data as we have for the nineteenth century show that the average size generally remained within five persons per household. There were no doubt spectacular examples where four or even five generations of persons lived under a single roof, but they could not have been very common if the average size was under five. The legal conception of the joint family is quite misleading here, because even two brothers living together without any other persons might be considered legally a joint family so long as their property remained undivided.

One must not misread the implications of the facts noted above. Even where most households are of the simple rather than the extended type, most individuals may have experienced living in a joint household at some stage in their lives. This is because the Indian household goes typically through a developmental cycle in which small and simple units expand into large and complex ones which in turn divide themselves into small and simple ones.

It cannot be argued that the joint family is declining in frequency and is likely to die out in the foreseeable future. The evidence shows that the proportion of joint households is as large, in both rural and urban areas, as it was a hundred and fifty years ago. There are of course variations between regions, between communities and between classes. It is perhaps in the service class, comprising administrators, managers and professionals, that the nuclear family shows its highest frequency. But even here, unlike in the West, the domestic unit rarely starts as a simple conjugal unit at marriage, but hives off after a period of incubation within a larger domestic unit.

There are changes, if not in size and outward form, at least in the texture of relations based on age and sex, particularly in the urban middle-class household. The most notable change in the last hundred years is the secular increase in the age at marriage for women in all communities and all social classes. Even in a joint family, it makes all the difference whether a new bride comes in at the age of twenty-two, or even eighteen, or at the age of twelve. Fewer children are being born, and more persons live to be old or very old, seeing their grandchildren mature and marry. Thus, even where the proportion between extended and nuclear households remains roughly what it was a hundred years ago, the family is no longer the same social unit that it was in the past.

At the same time, it is different and likely to remain different from the modern Western family. In India, yuppies and radicals alike are much more conservative in regard to family values than their Western counterparts. The kin group is more actively involved in the marriage of a person, even when it is not an arranged marriage, than in the West. Here the family is not a discrete or self-contained unit to nearly the same extent as in Europe or America. This is seen in our kinship terminology where we do not make the same kind of distinction between cousins and brothers (or sisters) that is made in the West. It is this anchorage in the wider kinship unit that gives to the Indian family many of its distinctive features as well as its continuing vitality.

20

Privacy and Secrecy

Indians place very little value on privacy; at the same time, they delight in secrecy. It may well be that the disregard of privacy and the fascination for secrecy are two sides of the same coin. One might say, of course, that these are questions of individual disposition. But the disposition towards privacy is encouraged in some societies and discouraged in others. So they are also questions of how societies are organized and cultures constituted.

The desire for privacy, which may be little more than the desire to be by oneself at certain places and certain times, is in our kind of society viewed with suspicion or at best treated as an oddity. I may give an example from my own experience in a south Indian village where I lived for ten months some thirty-five years ago in order to make a study of it.

In the village I lived in a rented room which had a cot, a swing and a tin trunk containing most of my worldly belongings. The work I did was demanding, both physically and emotionally, so I felt I needed a break from my investigations in the middle of the day. After my midday meal, I would lie down on my cot for an hour or so in my room upstairs. About a month into my work, I found that a young man of the village, from a good family but with no definite

The Telegraph, 27 October 1998.

occupation, would come up to the room every afternoon with his mat, spread it out by the side of my cot, and go to sleep. This daily routine of his made me feel acutely uneasy.

After some time and with some hesitation, I decided to bring the matter to the attention of my local patron, an influential Brahmin landowner with some college education. He at once took my side, said he knew the young man concerned, that he was lazy and good for nothing, a gossip and a chatterbox, and that he would stop him at once from pestering me while I was engaged in serious work. I was taken aback and said that my afternoon visitor did not try to engage me in any conversation, but just slept. My patron then said that he understood exactly what the matter was: the young man must be snoring very loudly, and that was bound to disturb my reading and writing. Being an honest man, I had to say that the young man did not snore, but only slept.

This exchange went on for a while. Finally, it was my patron's turn to express surprise. My visitor did not make much noise; he did not pilfer; he did not even ask me for money: what then was my problem? My problem, I tried to explain, was that I wanted to be by myself for a while in the afternoons; but I could see that my explanation did not carry any conviction. I might feel that my privacy was being invaded, but according to the moral code of the community in which I lived, I was just being selfish.

Sometimes the disregard of privacy comes as a boon to the outsider. The Japanese anthropologist Chie Nakane was not so much inconvenienced as puzzled by her experience of it. The Japanese do not have the kind of extensive kinship networks that the Indians and the Chinese do, and, on the testimony of Professor Nakane, they place a certain value on privacy within the domestic domain. When she came to stay in a village in West Bengal in the 1950s, she discovered that no such value was placed there. A young unmarried woman of the village, whom she befriended, took her not only to her own home, but to various other homes in which she moved about freely and easily, showing her the contents of cupboards and store-rooms without so much as asking anybody's permission. She explained that they were all related to her in one way or another and would naturally be delighted to have her Japanese friend see all the nice things they possessed. Nakane was astonished as a Japanese, but delighted as an anthropologist.

What this means perhaps is that different cultures promote different conceptions of the individual as a person. It has been said that in India, the person is open and connected whereas in the West, he is bounded and discreet. Western man builds an invisible wall around himself. It is not that there are no relations with others; but the limits of those relations are well defined and carefully kept in mind. There, one person is clearly distinct from the other. In India, on the other hand, the boundaries of the individual as a person are generally kept open, so that the lives of the individual members of the family, the kin group and the community flow easily into each other. These contrasts should not be overdrawn, but their existence cannot be denied.

No doubt the differences to which I have drawn attention are related to the fact that India is predominantly agricultural whereas the West is predominantly industrial (as is Japan). What I am trying to say, however, is that industrialization probably heightened the contrast but did not create it. The basic difference in orientation existed before the Industrial Revolution began in the West (and in Japan), and it will probably continue to exist even while India becomes progressively industrialized. There is no reason to believe that modernization will end by making all societies identical. The English, the Dutch, the Germans and others value privacy;

Indians, Pakistanis and Indonesians like to be gregarious. It would be absurd to argue that privacy ranks higher than gregariousness in any absolute scale of values.

A society in which the person is open and connected has its own internal strains. While society exerts pressure on the individual to be open and connected, nobody can in fact be open and connected all the time. Secrecy becomes the natural defence against the excessive demands of gregariousness. People who are obliged to live in each other's pockets develop a special urge to be secretive; those who are able to maintain their privacy in the ordinary course do not need to be secretive to the same extent.

The disapproval of privacy and the fascination for secrecy may be seen to coexist happily in any large Indian family. In such a family, every member is supposed to be open with every other member, and even kin terms are wilfully mixed up, so that the aunt is a mother, the uncle a father, and the cousins are brothers and sisters. Yet secrets have a luxuriant subterranean life, and their flow is guided along well-marked channels.

The same pattern may be seen on a larger scale in the extended kin group and in the community as a whole. The habit of secrecy is infectious and it becomes an end in itself. Mature and middle-aged persons make secrets of the most trivial matters, many of which are matters of common knowledge. Secrecy seeps into every social arrangement where it acts as a counterpoint to the open display of mutual affection expected of everyone. This is an age-old pattern in India, and no doubt it will adapt itself successfully to urbanization, industrialization and modernization.

IV
The Indian Identity

India's social and cultural identity is both diverse and dynamic. It varies enormously across space and has changed continuously over time. Any attempt to fit it into a single straitjacket is destined to be a failure. India has a rich and ancient tradition, but it is also a part of the modern world. Respect for tradition should not lead to a glorification of the past, and a living tradition does not need to insulate itself from the winds of change or to feel that it will be blown away by them.

The Indian cultural tradition tolerated and even encouraged great social diversity. In that sense it was pluralist in its orientation, but the diversity was organized hierarchically and not democratically. Pluralism is not the same thing as liberalism which, in addition to encouraging diversity, also gives a high value to the freedom of individual choice. Traditional Indian society was a society of castes and communities rather than of individuals.

Today India has little choice but to be a part of the modern world. The process of modernization is not a painless one. It creates divisions and tensions, but there is little evidence that Indian society is becoming polarized, with one part adhering blindly to tradition and the other equally blindly embracing modernity.

21

Diversity and Unity

The most striking feature of India's social and cultural heritage is its diversity. The People of India Project of the Anthropological Survey of India has identified a multitude of tribes, castes, sects and communities, each characterized by its own distinctive way of life. Many anthropologists have recorded in detail the inexhaustible variety in the habits, practices and customs of the people of India. There is first the diversity in material traits such as food, dress, habitation and the material arts and crafts. This is matched by the diversity of social institutions, and of religious beliefs and practices.

In India there is endless variety in the types of food eaten and in their preparation. Some of this variation can be easily ascribed to variations in the types of food grown under different geographical conditions. But these simple variations were subjected to infinite elaboration through the action of customs, conventions, rituals and other social prescriptions and interdictions whose operation had little to do with the known facts of geography. Then, there are variations in dress, habitation and the material arts and crafts that may be noted not only between regions but also within a region and, indeed, sometimes even within a single village.

Side by side, there are differences in social relations and

The Asian Age, 3 March 1997.

social institutions such as those associated with family, marriage, kinship, inheritance, succession and residence. Writing about the diversity characteristic of Indian society, the noted anthropologist and writer Irawati Karve observed, 'The variety of family organizations is equally great. Polygamy and polyandry are both found. There are groups which are matrilineal, and others which are patrilineal. The taboo on consanguine marriages changes from region to region and from caste to caste . . . The modes of inheritance and succession are also different.'

There is finally the inexhaustible multiplicity of religious beliefs and practices. Within Hinduism itself, one can pass from the crudest worship of sticks and stones to the most profound speculation about the nature and significance of the universe. But Hinduism is not the only religion of India. In addition to its offshoots Jainism, Buddhism and Sikhism, other religions such as Islam and Christianity have also made their home in the country. It is not at all uncommon to find even in the rural areas small local communities in which not only Hindus with various beliefs and practices but also Muslims and Christians pursue and maintain their distinctive ways of life.

The heritage of India has been built out of many components. This becomes evident when we look at its linguistic and religious diversity. New components, whether from within or outside, have been continuously accommodated throughout history. In being accommodated, these components acquired new orientations, but their old identities were not allowed to lapse.

Accommodation without assimilation has been the characteristic of Indian civilization until modern times. Adding new components has not meant discarding old ones, so that new and old components of the most heterogeneous kind have existed cheek-by-jowl to a far greater extent than elsewhere. Irawati Karve put the matter thus: 'The historical process is one of continuous accretion. There does not seem to be a stage where a choice was made between alternatives, a choice involving acceptance of one alternative and a definite, final rejection of others.'

The presence of diversity has been more than a matter of mere existence. Here, according to most authorities, a decisive part has been played by the core values of Hinduism in shaping not only Hindu society specifically, but Indian society as a whole. Respect for the diversity of habits, customs and practices of the people was enjoined not only by Hindu religion but also by Hindu law. There is a maxim of Yagnyavalka that says that 'one should not practice that which, though ordained by the Smriti, is condemned by the people'. P.V. Kane's monumental *History of Dharmasastra* gives a vivid account of the extraordinary maze of law, custom and usage by which social life was regulated in the past. In modern times, this extraordinary maze has been the nightmare of all those who have sought to bring some uniformity into the personal laws of Indians.

The polymorphous structure of Hindu society and its pluralist, not to say polytheist, cultural tradition provide congenial conditions for the growth of democracy. Democracy favours a diversity of ends and is averse to a single plan of life for everyone; it supports a plurality of parties and interests and opposes the control of society and politics by one single group or type of group. In short, the building of democratic institutions in modern India is bound to benefit from its long tradition of diversity and accommodation in social and cultural life.

It is not sufficient to take note of the remarkable accommodation of diversity in traditional India, it is also necessary to ask how this diversity was organized and held together. To put it in a nutshell, its organization was hierarchical and not democratic.

The Indian tradition was not only the most pluralistic known to human history, it was also the most hierarchical. While styles of life of the widest variety were acknowledged and accommodated, they were not all equally esteemed. An elaborate ritual idiom served to express and reinforce social distinctions between superiors and inferiors. Not only was each group expected to persevere in its own style of life, but there were sanctions against the adoption by groups of inferior rank of symbols of status allowed to their superiors. The accommodation of diversity included the accommodation of untouchability.

Just as the accommodation of diversity did not go with equality, it also did not go with individual freedom. In the matter of social practice, the individual was subordinated to the group, the three principal ones being village, caste and family. Thus, while a great variety of occupational techniques, marriage practices and ritual procedures was present in society as a whole, no individual could choose from among these according to his own inclination or convenience. The actions of the individual were severely constrained by the rules and practices of the group into which he was born. India has been described as a land of 'the most inviolable organization by birth'; and here too the spirit of the old social order was antithetical to the spirit of democracy.

What is clear is that the old principles by which society has been governed for two thousand years and more are no longer adequate for maintaining either order or stability under modern conditions. There were no doubt disorder and instability at particular times and places in the past; but whatever their degree or extent, both inequality of status and the subordination of the individual to the group were, generally speaking, morally acceptable principles in the past. Such is no longer the case. The challenge today is to maintain the diversity and the spirit of accommodation inherited from the past while repudiating hierarchy and creating more spaces for individual freedom.

The constitution that was adopted in the wake of independence sought to base itself not only on new values but also on new norms or regulatory principles. Diversity on the plane of values, or the ends considered desirable by various members of society, is to be expected in any large society undergoing a major transformation, and its tolerance is healthy up to a point. But how far can a modern society accommodate a plurality of norms or regulatory rules that are not only diverse but unclear, ambiguous and mutually inconsistent?

Fifty years after independence, there is widespread anxiety today over the many problems with which our public institutions are beset—misuse of funds, lack of discipline, absenteeism, work stoppages, strikes, and so on. All of these are related in one way or another to the failure of regulatory rules. Allegations about the violation of rules have become endemic, and they lead to the creation of new rules which are in turn violated.

This leads us to turn our attention to two striking features of contemporary Indian society that manifest themselves in every public institution from the state down to the smallest government dispensary. The first is the drive to create rules of every kind and to the last detail; and the second is to disregard those very rules. My view is that the proliferation of rules and the disregard of rules are two sides of the same coin; and, further, that these two complementary tendencies are very deeply rooted in our traditional culture.

I would like to stress that I am dealing with a tendency that is deeply rooted in our culture, and not simply with the malfunctioning of governmental bureaucracy. The maze of rules is all-pervasive, and we can examine how it works in universities, research institutes, hospitals and many other institutions that have no direct connection with the government. There are many thoughtful and well-intentioned persons who are aware of this and disturbed by it, but seem unable to do very much about it. Committees set up to streamline procedures invariably create new rules, and then Irawati Karve's law comes into operation: the addition of new rules does not lead to the elimination of old ones; they are simply put into cold storage, to be taken out when required to trip up any unwary newcomer who tries to inject some dynamism into the system.

These considerations seem to lead to the conclusion that we have an orientation towards rules that is largely our own and that is strikingly different from the orientations characteristic of other cultures. Bankimchandra, the great nineteenth-century writer, was troubled by the tendency of some of his contemporaries to quote prescriptions from the shastras to support one or another reform they wished to promote. He found those prescriptions to be prolix, ambiguous and self-contradictory. He wrote, 'Indeed, it is not possible for any society to be fully regulated by all the prescriptions to be found in the shastras of Manu and the others. It is doubtful if ever, at any time, those prescriptions were fully operative in any society. Many of them are inoperable. Many, though operable, involve such hardships to man that they would drop out on their own. Many are mutually contradictory. If any society is ever destined to keep all these prescriptions in operation, such a society has indeed an evil destiny.' Those who are frustrated by the maze of rules in offices in post-independence India may gain some consolation from Bankim's reflections on the past.

How do people get things done in the face of this plethora of obsolete, unclear and inconsistent rules? They improvise, activate personal networks, and go about their business without paying too much attention to the rules. This probably is how they worked the system in the past, and this is how they try to work it today. But people lived mostly in small, face-to-face communities in the past. Fifty years after independence, they operate in a world that is organized in a very different way and on a very different scale. Is it possible to act effectively in this world without a radical change of orientation towards the regulatory rules of society?

22

India's Identity

It is natural for those who live in such a large and diverse country as ours to feel concerned about the nature of the Indian identity. This identity cannot be defined simply in geographical or demographic terms. Beyond the land and its inhabitants, there are beliefs, practices and institutions that acquire a life of their own as they are carried forward from one generation to the next. But as soon as we try to fix the Indian identity in social, cultural or civilizational terms, we find ourselves on shifting sands. It is obvious that not all the myriad elements that shape the lives of the people of India are equally enduring or equally significant. How are we to determine what constitutes the essential and authentic core of the Indian identity? And whose authority should prevail in the reckoning?

Today there are no social legislators, no *dharmadhikaris* with the intellectual and moral authority to determine what is essential and what is dispensable in the Indian way of life. No matter how much they agonize over questions of authenticity and integrity, our modern and post-modern intellectuals lack the conviction to lay down the law about the Indian way of life in a clear and categorical way. But

The Telegraph, 9 July 1998.

their anxieties can induce others with more political vigour and less delicate sensibilities to press for one or another plan of life as the only authentically Indian one.

No matter how we perceive or represent India's identity today, two kinds of interconnections have to be kept in view. The first is the connection with our past; the second is the connection with our contemporaries elsewhere, in other parts of the world. Our orientation to our own past and our orientation to our contemporaries outside together shape our beliefs and practices here and now. These two orientations make divergent demands on our intellectual, moral and political capacities, and it will be naïve to presume that those demands can be easily harmonized.

In a country whose civilization has withstood the passage of so many centuries, it is natural to look to the past as a source and a guarantor of present identity. It is easy to pick out examples of beliefs and practices carried over from the past into the present in virtually every field: material culture, social arrangements, religious ritual and ceremony. It is far more difficult to represent these various beliefs and practices as a coherent unity. Part of the difficulty arises from the fact that the various components that make up the Indian tradition are not all of the same provenance or all equally old: some go back to the ancient past while others are of much more recent origin.

It is true that all civilizations build traditions through the incorporation of various elements from diverse sources. But the growth of Indian civilization was based on a very distinctive pattern of accommodation which the noted anthropologist and writer Irawati Karve described as a process of continuous accretion. She observed, 'The historical process is one of continuous accretion. There does not seem to be a stage where a choice was made between alternatives, a choice involving acceptance of one alternative and a definite, final rejection of the other.' This process was sustained by a remarkable tolerance of diversity, not only in religious beliefs and practices but also in moral and legal codes.

There is no harm in invoking tradition as a source and guarantor of our identity, provided we keep two things in mind. First, in a country such as ours there are many traditions, and the idea of one single tradition as the guarantor of our true identity should not be used to iron out the many distinctive features of particular identities. Second, tradition should not be equated with sheer antiquity. A tradition is not necessarily less compelling because its origins do not go back to the distant past. In contemporary societies, the traditions of scientific research or of parliamentary democracy do not go further back than a couple of hundred years; they are traditions nevertheless.

Traditions do not always grow entirely on their own. They are given shape and form by the conscious, not to say self-conscious, efforts of the reflective members of society. Sometimes these efforts are deliberate and calculative, and we may then speak of the invention or even the fabrication of tradition. By and large, those who have sought to define the Indian identity by looking backward have tended to privilege the distant over the recent past. Adopting such a stance has its own advantage: since our knowledge of the distant past is highly fragmentary, there is more room for the play of artifice in deciding what that past was like. But in the end it becomes difficult to sustain the position that new traditions ceased to take shape in India with the establishment of Muslim rule in medieval times or of British rule in modern times. On the contrary, Indian ways of life and thought have been significantly reshaped through the continuous incorporation of elements from Western as well as Islamic culture.

Those who are jealous of the unity and integrity of India are anxious about the threat to its authentic way of life from dominant and seductive beliefs and practices of alien origin. This anxiety is expressed by many traditional and some post-modern intellectuals in our time. Traditionalists warn against the threat to the purity of our age-old way of life posed by un-Indian beliefs and practices. Post-modernists remain constantly on guard against the penetration of the collective Self by the sinister Other. Traditionalists and post-modernists find a common ground in their suspicions and misgivings about the modern world in which we are all condemned to live.

Even in ancient and medieval times, there was a measure of interpenetration among civilizations. But the diffusion and accommodation of beliefs and practices took place in slow motion, so that it was relatively easy to sustain the illusion that each civilization was a world unto itself. That illusion has now become impossible to sustain. Human beings everywhere are now more exposed to the external world than they ever were in the past. They are able to participate more actively and more vividly, in reality and in the imagination, in the lives of their contemporaries across the globe than their ancestors were. Despite all the bitterness and the violence that surrounds us today, the expansion of the capacity for human sympathy is a striking feature of the modern world.

Our dependence on a wider and more contemporary moral environment and not merely on the resources of the past becomes evident when we look at our constitution which may be seen as the blueprint for Indian society. We have had such blueprints in the past in the broad class of texts known as the Dharmashastra. It would be difficult to argue that the ideals that animate our present constitution owe more to the ideals of the Dharmashastra than to other modern constitutions. What applies to the Constitution of India applies to the entire legal order by which our present lives are governed or expected to be governed.

To be sure, not all are satisfied with every feature of our present constitution and our present legal system. Changes are being continuously made in both, and demands are put forward for further and more radical changes. In the search for more appropriate ideas than those in the present constitution, we might recover some nuggets—relating to, say, community or consensus—from our ancient and medieval past, but it will be foolish for that reason to turn our backs on ideas taking shape before our eyes, so to say, in other parts of the contemporary world. Even the most radical critics of the present legal order use arguments that seem suspiciously similar to those in current use elsewhere, particularly in the Western world.

The constitutional and legal order created in the wake of independence was the culmination of a process of modernization that had been in operation for the previous hundred years. That process established new beliefs and new practices. Therefore, when we speak today of our identity, our institutions and even our traditions, it will be disingenuous to invoke only our distant past and to ignore or neglect what was attempted and achieved in the last hundred and fifty years.

The modernization of India was by no means a painless process; it inflicted many wounds that remain open to this day. In the institutional domain, what was achieved fell far short of what was attempted. Many new institutions—civic bodies, universities, even political parties—which began promisingly, now seem to be falling apart. Yet they too have become a part of our Indian identity, and we cannot wish them out of existence. Fifty years after independence, it has become more rather than less common among our intellectuals to attribute our failures to our moral and intellectual dependence on the West. The milder and more reasonable critique of westernization has been displaced by a more strident and intransigent onslaught on that mysterious entity called 'post-Enlightenment modernity'.

No matter how greatly civilizations might benefit by the interchange of beliefs and practices, this interchange does not take place on terms of equality. In any given historical epoch, some civilizations play a more active and others a more passive role in it. This was no doubt the case even in the past, but the lack of parity between the West and the rest has become increasingly manifest and, in many eyes, increasingly odious in our time. Therefore, there is a resistance to the adoption of even beneficial elements from the West, if only because the terms of the interchange are so unequal.

The Indian identity may be regarded as being more or less open to penetration and alteration by influences from outside. Some regard those influences as being on the whole beneficial while others regard them as being sinister and debilitating. Those who welcome the forces of modernization, from no matter which quarter, do not by any means disown or disparage all that has come down from the past. Likewise, those who would like India to do its own thing without being disturbed by temptations from outside, particularly the West, do not necessarily wish the country to remain frozen in a timeless mould. They too want India to be modern, but they want it to be modern in its own way. They too value democracy, but they yearn for India to be democratic in an authentically Indian way. They want equality, liberty and a secular social order, but they want all these things in their definitive Indian forms. And if there are no definitive Indian forms of the things they desire, then they would rather wait for them to be invented at home than adapt to their own use what is already available abroad.

23

Two Indias?

The carnage in Gujarat that followed the brutal assault on a railway bogie at Godhra has sent shock waves throughout the country. It is not simply that the reprisals were widespread and continuous or that the state allowed and in some sense even encouraged the violence. Even more shocking than the complicity of the state is the evidence from reliable and responsible citizens of Gujarat that large numbers of their fellow citizens felt that the reprisals were justified and well deserved. At such a juncture one begins to wonder where to draw the line between the normal and the pathological or indeed whether such a line can at all be drawn in contemporary India.

Liberal, secular and cosmopolitan Indians outside Gujarat —and perhaps also in Gujarat—have begun to ask whether the India they had constructed in their own image may not be a fantasy. They are beginning to wonder if the real India is not the one that has shown its face in Gujarat and may show it elsewhere too: illiberal, intolerant, hidebound, vengeful and without any respect for the rule of law. They feel that perhaps the kind of society envisaged in the constitution cannot strike roots in India because its supporters are too few and its opponents too many.

The Telegraph, 5 June 2002.

This mood of despair will hopefully pass. At the same time, the idea that there are two Indias, in uneasy if not unhappy coexistence in the same land, is both widespread and deep-rooted. A homespun expression of that idea is in the contrast between India and Bharat. In this contrast it is often the latter with its eternal and steadfast values that is represented as superior to the artificial and borrowed lifestyles presumed to characterize the former. The contrast is commonly made in these terms by Indians who are themselves modern and cosmopolitan to their fingertips. India's modernizing elite likes to add spice to its life with a generous dose of self-hatred.

It needs no social theorist to point out that Indian society is highly differentiated not only in terms of language, region, religion and caste, but also in terms of literacy, education, occupation and class. Vast numbers of Indians are governed less by the rule of law than by the rules of caste and community. For centuries India has been a society of castes and communities rather than of citizens. The creation of citizenship and the kind of modern institutions that alone can ensure its effective operation can hardly be a swift or painless process. Yet to abandon the endeavour after having gone so far along the road and to turn backwards would lead to disorder and violence on a scale we can scarcely imagine.

Democracy finds itself at odds with the kind of caste- and community-based hierarchical society we inherited from the past. Bharat has to be brought forward into the modern age for democracy to work successfully in India. No one saw this more clearly than Dr B.R. Ambedkar who had said in the Constituent Assembly: 'Democracy in India is only a top-dressing on an Indian soil, which is essentially undemocratic.' For a modern secular and democratic society to come into its own, many things inherited from the past have to go, and they do not all go easily. The social arrangement of various castes and communities worked after a fashion in a static society in which they more or less accepted their allotted places. It cannot work in the same way in a dynamic and changing society where their places are no longer fixed.

The processes of economic, political and social change have in the last fifty years unsettled old arrangements and introduced new disparities. There is already a large and expanding middle class, and there are millions of persons in cities, towns and even villages waiting to join that class. Those who have enjoyed socially secure positions in it for three or four generations may occasionally yearn for the lost world of their ancestors, but there are countless other less fortunate and less experienced persons who are eager to taste the sweets of middle-class existence. The appeal of that kind of existence is not confined to only those who have opted for India; it extends also to those who are presumed to stand for Bharat.

My aim is not to maintain that modern Indian society is made of whole cloth or that there are no cracks or fissures running across it. It is only to point out that the modernizing elite and the socially disadvantaged masses do not constitute two nations, any more than Hindus and Muslims, or north Indians and south Indians, or Dwijas and Shudras do. There are many cleavages in Indian society, but they do not all run along the same line. This means that there are not only cleavages—of language, religion, education, occupation, and so on—but also cross-cutting ties. Political expediency might lead interested parties to focus upon one single cleavage while ignoring all the others, but polarization, no matter how destructive in the short run, is at odds with the basic design of Indian society.

Far less than in the case of language, religion or caste is

there any clear line of division separating the educated middle class from the rest of Indian society. Those who pursue modern, secular and cosmopolitan lifestyles and those whose lives are governed by the traditional values of caste and community do not live in distinct watertight compartments. Not only are there many linkages of family, kinship and marriage between persons at different stages of modernity, but very liberal and highly conservative orientations to society and politics may be found in one and the same individual.

There are many differences between India's modernizing elite and the rest of Indian society. But one must not exaggerate the differences or ignore the many linkages between the two. For one thing, the elite is not a unity with a homogeneous style of life or even a singular conception of modernity; and the rest of Indian society follows many different traditions, varying with region, religion and caste. It is not true that modern values such as those attached to technological progress, success in competition and respect for impersonal rules are simply imposed from above by a minuscule minority of secular and westernized intellectuals and that they raise no echoes in the rest of the population.

Millions of Indians, whether urban or rural and whether highly or only moderately educated, want modern technology and modern education. There are no doubt some hypersensitive intellectuals who never cease to complain about the alienating effects of a modern education on the Indian psyche. But that does not prevent them from arranging for their children to have precisely that kind of education, and then trying, if possible, to send them to Harvard or Princeton which one might suspect to be even more alienating than Modern School or St Stephen's College. A modern education is valued by all, irrespective of ideological orientation. Indians are given to talking much about values in the abstract. But their real values are revealed in the plans they make for the education and employment of their children. As far as that goes, India and Bharat seem to vote in the same way.

24

The Politics of Resentment

The disintegration of the Congress party has by now come to be accepted by many Indians with resignation. To those who believed that the Congress was not just a political party but a part of India's national heritage, this must be a cause for some sorrow. Many factors have contributed to the disintegration: corruption from top to bottom; indiscipline at every level; and the sheer ineptitude and lethargy of its ageing leadership. Symptomatic of all this is the leadership's paralysis in the face of even the most trivial sorts of crisis in interpersonal relations.

Many persons in Delhi have begun to think of the BJP as the successor to the Congress on the Indian political scene. But it is doubtful that the BJP will emerge as a national party of the kind that the Congress has been. It is and is destined to remain a great regional party. It is easy enough to accept that the DMK, the TDP and the AGP are regional parties. It is a little more difficult to accept that the CPM is a regional party, but that is what it is, for West Bengal and for Kerala. The BJP too is a regional party whose character as one is obscured by the vast extent and population of the region in which it has its home.

Since independence, the smaller parties have developed

their distinctive cultures. This has perhaps received less attention than it deserves. The DMK has developed its own political culture which has its roots in the Dravidian movement of E.V. Ramaswami Naicker; the AIADMK participates in the same general political culture, which is natural since it began as an offshoot of the former. It is a different political culture from that of the CPM, whether in West Bengal or in Kerala. I have been struck during my visits to Calcutta and its environs by the manner in which the politics of the state of West Bengal and its culture have adapted to each other. The BJP has developed a different and a distinctive political culture, and I find it difficult to believe that it will find a congenial home in either West Bengal or Tamil Nadu.

Too much is made by anxious secular intellectuals in Delhi and Calcutta of the BJP's intransigent hostility to Islam. If I were to sum up the BJP's political culture in a single phrase, it is 'Hindu *bano*, Hindi *bolo*'. I first heard that phrase twenty years ago in the aftermath of the Emergency, and it has remained engraved in my mind. In the great Hindi-speaking region of the country, it has an immediate appeal for all political parties, but it is the BJP that can articulate the sentiment behind it most effectively. The Congress has a different past which it cannot shake off very easily.

If it were only a matter of Hindutva, the BJP would be able to spread its influence without too much trouble. After all, more than 80 per cent of Indians are Hindus, of one sort or another. What would be the problem in adding Shiv and Durga, or even the Pir Satyanarayan, to Ram? But persuading people to embrace Hindi may be more difficult than persuading them to remain Hindu. Heir though he is to a great atheist tradition, Mr Karunanidhi will be more at ease in a Hindu temple than at a political rally where all the slogans are in Hindi. And this may turn out to be true for the vast majority of Indians outside inner India.

Whereas Hindus make up more than 80 per cent of the population, Hindi speakers do not add up to more than 40 per cent by even the most liberal estimate. This must surely be a source of anxiety to the leaders of a political party identified so closely not only with the Hindu religion but also with the Hindi language. Will they not do something about it that will give their party a different direction and a different image? I believe that they can do very little. In the age of mass democracy, it is easier to alter a party's political programme than to alter its political culture.

The difference of political culture between the BJP and the CPM is only partly a matter of political ideology; it is also a matter of regional culture. It will be difficult to deny that the region that has provided the most congenial environment for the growth and consolidation of the BJP is a backward region. It is backward on every significant count: demographic, economic and educational. The resistance of Bihar, Madhya Pradesh, Rajasthan and Uttar Pradesh—the BIMARU states as they are sometimes called—to development and modernization is notorious, and needs no further elaboration. What may perhaps be stressed is the irony that by far the largest and most populous region in the country is also the most backward. This provides a built-in depressant against the modernization of the country.

Secularists like to frighten themselves with the thought that as soon as the BJP comes to power in New Delhi, it will start a massacre of the Muslims. It is unlikely to do that. Mr Vajpayee as prime minister will be no less interested in the maintenance of law and order than Mr Narasimha Rao—but no more effective. It is doubtful that the BJP will have either a radically different economic policy or a radically different foreign policy. What it is likely to hit hardest is education where, apart from the opportunity to distribute patronage widely, there is the bonus for demanding the expulsion of English. 'Angrezi hatao' expresses hostility not just to the English language but to a whole system and method of education. Fortunately, education is largely a state subject, so whether or not the BJP comes to power at the centre, the damage will not be equally extensive everywhere.

The BJP is better poised than any other party to transfer the politics of backwardness from the plane of caste to the regional plane. Not that the demands of the backward castes will disappear, but they will be accommodated within a larger scheme in which backwardness, and not caste as such, will provide the basic energy for the mobilization of political support. The principal targets of attack will be those things that stand for progress and modernity in education and culture. This will affect economic development only indirectly, for those who feel threatened by liberal modern culture are by no means all averse to the material gains from improved technology and more profitable international trade.

The politics of backwardness is different in its tone and texture from the politics of the proletariat. It is above all a politics of resentment. In India today there is resentment against a great many things, and not just the Brahmins or even the upper castes. Mr Mani Shankar Aiyar, in dissociating himself from the Congress party, lamented the shabby treatment of the educated classes at the hands of its present leadership. That has now become a general feature of Indian politics, but it will acquire a particular emphasis in the Hindi heartland because of its backwardness. Here the BJP has a clear advantage, for its target of attack is not just Islam, but the modern world, including its secular intellectuals.

25

Pluralism and Liberalism

The Indian cultural tradition is a pluralist tradition, it is not a liberal one. The great variety of castes, sects and communities that make up the larger society have been allowed or even encouraged to practise their diverse ways of life since time immemorial. But the freedom of individual choice, not to speak of individual dissent, has been limited. Diversity of practice was allowed between groups, but not between individuals within the same group. The freedom of the individual to act in his own way was kept in check not so much by the state or its agents as by the community of which he was a member by birth and within which he remained embedded. The current resurgence of identity politics, or the politics of caste and community, is but an expression of the primacy of the group over the individual. It does not augur well for liberal democracy in India.

The tolerance of diversity has been a byword with those, whether from within or outside the country, who have written about Indian civilization in the past. Hinduism is a polytheistic religion which has grown by accommodating diverse beliefs and practices even when they were not always mutually consistent. Nor was the accommodation of diversity confined only to religion. A multitude of languages and

The Hindu, 4 January 2002.

dialects continues to be in existence to this day, and Indian society is undoubtedly the most polyglot one in the world. Even very small speech communities maintain their identity in the midst of very large ones. Diversity of religion, sect, language and dialect has gone hand in hand with diversity of food, dress, habitation, marriage rules, family patterns and styles of life in general. Accommodation without assimilation appears to have been the guiding principle of Indian society from the very beginning.

Diversity in ways of life came to be organized in a particular way which ensured that it was reproduced from generation to generation. Family, caste and community became the repositories of the diverse ways of life prevalent in society. Fidelity to custom and the established way of life became the responsibility of neither the individual nor society as a whole, but of the community. Fidelity to a way of life and loyalty to one's community of birth became two sides of the same coin. In course of time the great diversity of habits, practices and customs came to be matched by a great multiplicity of tribes, clans, castes, sects and other communities. On the cultural side, India is unmatched for its diversity of customs and usages; on the social side, it is unmatched for its multiplicity of castes and communities.

Colonial administrators were fascinated by the castes and communities they encountered everywhere in India, among Hindus, Sikhs, Muslims and even Christians. Perhaps they were not wholly wrong in believing that caste was in some sense even more important than religion, for it survived conversion from one religion to another. In the north, Jats did not cease to be Jats when they converted to Sikhism or Islam; and in the south, the Nadars did not cease to be Nadars when they converted to Christianity. The ICS anthropologists were inclined to believe that India was a society not of individuals but of castes and communities. They set about identifying, enumerating and classifying all the different castes and communities that make up the mosaic of Indian society. In this process they probably heightened to some degree the awareness of the differences of caste and community in the minds of people. But it would be a travesty to say that those divisions themselves were the creation of colonial rule; they were an integral part of the social structure long before the British came.

While strengthening the consciousness of caste in some respects, British rule also introduced a liberal impulse into Indian society by creating institutions and professions which required individuals to be treated on merit without consideration of caste and community. This liberal impulse found its way into the nationalist movement by the end of the nineteenth century. Many of the leaders of that movement, such as Motilal Nehru, G.K. Gokhale and C.R. Das were men of a genuinely liberal disposition who wanted to create a public domain in which individuals would be free from the prejudices of caste and community. But they perhaps misjudged the strength of the currents against which they were trying to carry their country forward.

The liberal spirit was clearly in evidence in the Constituent Assembly which sought to create a charter for a 'casteless and classless' society with strong rights of citizenship for the individual. Some felt then that nothing should be allowed to stand between the individual at one end and the nation at the other to the detriment of individual freedom and national solidarity. But the divisions of caste and community did not disappear with the attainment of independence, the partition of the country and the adoption of a modern, liberal constitution. They remained dormant until woken to new life by political forces that became increasingly assertive after the Emergency.

The Mandal Commission, set up after the Emergency was lifted, became a kind of turning point. It legitimized on an unprecedented scale the use of caste and community in the name of social justice. The Commission's list of Other Backward Classes was made up of 3,743 communities arranged by state and union territory. A decade or so later, the People of India Project of the Government of India made a list of 6,748 communities out of which 4,635 had been investigated and described by the early 1990s. Again, these divisions were not created *ex nihilo* by the Mandal Commission or the Anthropological Survey of India, just as the colonial administration did not create out of nothing the castes and communities that they made their obsession. But there can be no doubt that the operations referred to have since 1977 given new strength and vigour to identity politics at every level: national, regional and local.

Identity politics alters people's perceptions of themselves and of others. Larger identities tend to split into smaller ones, and those into yet smaller ones. At the grass-roots level, it tends to range caste against caste and, within the same caste, sub-caste against sub-caste. Rivalries between communities are reinforced or created anew, and social justice, the ostensible basis of identity politics, recedes into the background. The erection of statues and the naming of districts or streets or public buildings become objects of bitter contention between castes and communities. Such contention, encouraged by identity politics, makes people increasingly sensitive to the honour, dignity and reputation of their respective communities and their leaders. Detached observers and commentators are cowed into accepting the exalted opinions of the community expressed by its own leaders for fear of provoking an agitation or even a riot.

The recent contention over the sanitization of school textbooks has brought to the surface the illiberal consequences of identity politics and the obsession with caste and community on which it feeds. The matter has been represented in the press as a struggle between the left and the right, but that is only the tip of the iceberg. Passages are being deleted because one or another community has represented that its honour has been impugned therein. Such representations are likely to multiply in the future. Political leaders are helpless in their face because they have implicated themselves so deeply in identity politics. Nor are politicians alone responsible for this state of affairs. Intellectuals of various complexions have endorsed identity politics in the mistaken belief that in India that is the royal road to social justice. They have given little thought to what such politics can do to the dissenting voices of individual scholars or writers. Here there is neither left nor right but sheer political opportunism and intellectual muddle.

Liberal intellectuals have in any case to swim against the current in a society where the community is valued so much above the individual. Their friends from the left and the right should not make things needlessly difficult for them by adopting postures about social justice and the political obligations of the intellectual.

26

Modernity and Tradition

When decolonization began more than fifty years ago, it was widely believed that the world was divided into two types of society, the traditional and the modern. This division corresponded almost exactly with the division between underdeveloped and developed countries. The optimists believed that, with appropriate policy interventions, the underdeveloped countries would cease to be underdeveloped; and a well-known study of the 1950s recorded, with evident satisfaction, what it called 'the passing of traditional society'. The modernization of society became an important objective in many, if not most, of the newly independent countries. Soon it became evident that modernization has costs as well as benefits, and sometimes the costs might outweigh the benefits. The decline of tradition takes many things of value away with it, and the enthusiasm for modernization brings in unforeseen problems.

Is there any society in the world which is wholly traditional without any trace of modernity? Is there any which is so modern that it is now wholly free from tradition? France is by any account a modern society, but the French are proud, not to say jealous, of their traditions. Indian society is steeped in tradition, but that does not mean that Indians care nothing for modernity and modernization. Indeed, the hunger for modernization is very widespread in India, even in the rural areas, although intellectuals with refined sensibilities might find the peasant's appetite for it somewhat disconcerting.

The enthusiasm for modernization may be seen in combination with a regard for tradition in the speeches and writings of independent India's first prime minister. Jawaharlal Nehru was a committed modernizer, yet he placed a high value on the heritage of India. But when he spoke and wrote about tradition, what he chiefly had in mind were art, architecture, music, literature and philosophy, rather than the customs that form the basis of everyday social life. A society can modernize and still carry forward its traditions of art, literature and philosophy; how far it can do so while retaining its archaic and oppressive social customs is a different question.

It is in fact very easy to combine the pursuit of modernity with a nostalgia for tradition. The person who had little nostalgia for tradition was Dr B.R. Ambedkar. For him tradition stood not so much for high culture and art as for oppressive social custom. Ambedkar was a democrat who put his trust in equality and individual freedom, and he saw little of either in the Indian social tradition. 'Democracy in India,' he said in the Constituent Assembly, 'is a top-dressing on an Indian soil, which is essentially undemocratic.' By the 'Indian soil' he meant mainly the substratum of the traditional social structure and life as it was lived in the Indian village.

It is a mistake to think of tradition as a unitary phenomenon or to believe that modernization follows a uniform course that leads to the same outcome everywhere. Not all 'traditional societies' have social and cultural traditions of the same kind, and not all 'modern societies' are modern in the same way. Traditional ways change all the time, and what appear as technical or institutional innovations become established as traditions in course of time.

Although it may be misleading to characterize whole societies as either traditional or modern, certain attitudes and orientations are distinctive of modernity and modernization. The modern world seeks innovation and change actively and continuously; it is in that sense a restless world. It is not that societies never changed in the past, but change did not generally come from the conscious and deliberate effort at technical, organizational and institutional innovation. It is another matter that the innovations of today do not always bear fruit, or bear fruits that are very different from those envisaged.

What do modernity and modernization stand for? Nothing could be more tendentious than the view that modernity calls for the eradication of tradition. No society can survive, let alone prosper, if it turns its back on tradition as such. The modern man values tradition, but he does not place an absolute value on it. The traditionalist attaches overwhelming importance to what he believes to have existed since time immemorial. For him the past has an intrinsic value that it does not have for others.

The distinctive feature of modernity, as I understand it, is that it examines the world with an open and a sceptical mind. As I have said, no society can escape from its past; but a society should not remain tied inexorably to that past. No doubt, traditionalists believe that society can and should be improved. But they also believe that the ingredients for that improvement are to be found mainly, if not wholly, in their own social and cultural tradition. Tradition for them is a vast and inexhaustible storehouse having hidden, even unknown, treasures. One has only to dig deep enough to find all the ingredients for the regeneration of society at the present time. The traditionalist is averse to looking outwards among other contemporary societies for ingredients to rebuild society; he would rather look back again and again into his own past for that purpose.

The modernist is outward rather than backward looking. His primary engagement is with the contemporary world which includes not just his own society but other societies as well. His engagement with his own society is with its living traditions, good as well as bad, but not necessarily with everything that lies hidden and buried in the past. Modernity entails not just openness to innovation but also openness to the outside world. Every living tradition has, without exception, accommodated ingredients from other traditions. The present world allows this to be done openly and consciously to an unprecedented degree. The boundaries between different traditions were never watertight at any time, but they are far more porous now than ever before.

Not everything that appears attractive in other societies which have been active in technical or institutional innovation can be easily accommodated in one's own society. It is often the case in the contemporary world that countries that are less advanced economically imitate those that are more advanced blindly and mechanically without consideration of their needs or their capacity to absorb or integrate what they borrow. The pressures to catch up are continuous and relentless in our time. They often impel the leaders of society to act thoughtlessly and against its long-term interests. But blind and mechanical imitation is not an aid to modernization; it is an impediment to it.

Modernity calls for a sceptical attitude not only towards what has come down from the past but also towards what appears attractive at a distance. It does not accept without question that what prevails must be preserved because it is and has been for generations a part of our own way of life. Nor does it accept without question the view that success somewhere is a guarantee of success in every society, including one's own. It does not put a premium on other ways of life over one's own, but it recognizes that the ways of the past are also other ways of life, and not necessarily one's own way.

27

Modernity and Its Alternatives

The modernization of Indian society was a matter of central concern for those who assumed power when the country became independent more than fifty years ago. The intelligentsia as a whole viewed modernization with favour if not enthusiasm. This was true not only of India but of newly independent countries throughout the world. Decolonization was viewed as an opportunity not for a return to the past but for a more effective participation in the modern world. It was tacitly assumed that some countries had travelled further along the road to modernity than others but that the others too could and should catch up with the former.

The modernization of society was regarded as not only desirable for its own sake but also as a precondition for the development of the economy and the advance of democracy. Economic development was an urgent task in a country in which poverty and stagnation were widespread. Much of the blame for the poor state of the economy was laid at the door of colonial rule. With the removal of that constraint, the road to economic development seemed wide open. But there were internal constraints as well in the form of age-old social habits, practices, customs and institutions. In the newly independent countries of Asia and Africa, the obstacles to

The Hindu, 8 May 2002.

economic growth were not only technological, they were also institutional. The removal of those obstacles or the modernization of society was thus viewed as essential for growth and development.

The advance of democracy also required some recasting of traditional social arrangements. Indeed, the idea of 'political development' soon took its place by the side of economic development. The creation of democracy did not stop with the adoption of adult franchise and the holding of regular elections, important as they were. It required effective political socialization and political participation, in short, education in citizenship. Old attitudes of deference and submissiveness had to give place to new ones which enabled people to recognize their rights as citizens. This too called for the modernization of society.

The impulse for modernization came from many different sources and not just from the requirements of economic development and democratic politics. In the wake of independence, Indians looked forward to participating in the modern world as free and equal members. The political leadership under Nehru was modernist and not traditionalist. Independence created new opportunities for breaking free from the cobwebs of the past. The Indian middle class wanted a modern and not a traditional education for its children. The urge for a modern, not to say a Western, education for their children has expanded and intensified among middle-class families in the last fifty years.

The seeds of modernization, along with those of democracy and development, were planted in the Indian soil during the period of colonial rule. Independence and decolonization brought in new elements and new configurations, but at least in India, they did not lead to a break with the immediate past. Neither Jawaharlal Nehru, the first prime minister, nor

B.R. Ambedkar, the main architect of the new constitution, wanted such a break; and even Sardar Patel threw in his weight in favour of retaining the ICS, till then regarded as the steel frame of imperial rule.

Attitudes to modernity and modernization have changed between the middle of the twentieth century and the beginning of the twenty-first. Fifty years ago the modernists held the field because the traditionalists spoke in a weak voice and post-modernism was yet to be born. There are various reasons why modernization has lost some of the appeal it once enjoyed. First, as the process unfolded, its social costs became more and more apparent, and to some at least, they seemed to outweigh its benefits. In some areas and in certain phases it tends to increase rather than reduce the gap between the socially advantaged and the disadvantaged. Second, certain homogenizing tendencies inherent in modernization make it appear as a perpetual threat to the social and cultural identity of the nation as a whole, of rich and poor alike. The prophets of doom declare that modernization will rob Indian society and culture of its identity and yet leave Indians far behind on the path of progress.

Apprehensions of loss of identity are not easy to dispel; one can at best try to see that they do not assume pathological forms. In its origin and evolution the idea of modernization has been tied inextricably to that of westernization: that has been the poisoned chalice for many ardent nationalists who want their country to progress. Many might like to subscribe to modernization but they would not like to submit to Western hegemony. Is it possible to have a modernity that will be completely untainted by any association with Western ideas and values?

In an important study of the Arab world conducted just after decolonization began, Daniel Lerner spoke by preference of modernization rather than westernization. He explained his preference by saying that his Arab readers would be more comfortable with the first than with the second. They welcomed modernization but were deeply ambivalent towards the West.

In his Tagore lectures delivered barely a decade later, M.N. Srinivas decided to face the issue squarely and chose 'westernization' instead of 'modernization'. He pointed to the complexity of westernization and to the depth of its penetration in Indian society. Although it had spread widely, its spread was not uniform. It started during colonial rule, but the end of colonial rule did not bring westernization to an end. Rather, as Srinivas noted, 'the process has become greatly intensified, in many ways, since 1947 when India became independent'. Further, there was, according to him, a change in the motive force by which the process was driven. In the nineteenth century, the desire for social reform took precedence over the urge for national freedom, but the priorities became reversed in course of time.

Srinivas's account of social change in modern India, published in the mid-1960s, is remarkable for its depth of historical insight and its freedom from ideological cant. He gave its due share of credit to British rule but did not fail to point out that the British acted in their own interest which was not always the interest of their Indian subjects. Nor did he believe that 'the mindless imitation of the West' was all that there was to the process of westernization. Although by no means uncritically admiring of India's modernizing elite, he gave its members credit for their capacity for adaptation and innovation. 'Their role,' he said, 'was far from restricted to borrowing things, ideas and institutions from the British; the borrowing was selective and the borrowed item was subjected to elaboration and reinterpretation.' In this view, westernization appears as a process of 'creative destruction', although Srinivas did not use that phrase.

Indian society has moved too far along the road to modernity for it to be able to turn back now or even to stay at a standstill. No society can today opt out of the modern world without doing irreparable harm to itself. Being a part of the modern world means remaining open to influences from all around. There will be blind imitation, no matter how much we deplore it; but there will also be intelligent adaptation as there has been in the past. Too much anxiety about the loss of identity and authenticity puts brakes on a society's natural process of growth.

Modernization has not led all societies to become carbon copies—or caricatures—of any one society, and is unlikely to do so in the future. The modern world allows choices to be made, but the choices are not unrestricted. There are those who say that the modernity that emerged in the West in the wake of the Enlightenment is irredeemably flawed, and that we should turn our back on it and create our own alternative modernity. That would be a vain and hopeless pursuit. Modernization is not like a bus which one boards as one chooses and from which one alights as one pleases.

V
Inequality and Class

Indian society has been marked by deep and pervasive inequalities. The regime of caste was based on a multiplicity of castes and communities that were clearly divided from each other and arranged in an elaborate hierarchy.

The regime of caste has been seriously shaken by a new legal and economic order, but the inequalities due to caste have not disappeared altogether. While the divisions of caste are in decline, new forms of inequality based on wealth, income, occupation and education have begun to acquire prominence in society. The Indian middle class is today significant not only culturally, socially and politically but also demographically. It is also highly diverse, being divided first on the basis of occupation and education and next on the basis of language, religion and caste. There is, in addition, a large class of manual workers today. This class is also highly diverse, and those of its members who are in the organized sector now have many of the attributes of the middle class in terms of income and expenditure.

There is a great disjunction between professions of equality tirelessly made in public and social practice which is marked by inequalities of every kind. In a large, complex and dynamic society such as ours, inequality cannot be abolished but it can certainly be regulated and moderated.

28

The Promise of Equality

In the past Indian society was unique in the extremes to which it carried the principle and practice of inequality; today Indian intellectuals appear unique in their zeal for promoting the adoption of equality in every sphere of society. Marxists call for the liquidation of the class structure, feminists demand the abolition of patriarchy and citizens in general want to put an end to bureaucratic hierarchy. Most persons would place themselves on the side of equality, and few would like to speak of the limits to which it can be attained.

Nehru had said on the eve of independence, 'The spirit of the age is in favour of equality, though practice denies it almost everywhere'; and, being an optimist, had added, 'Yet the spirit of the age will triumph.' More than fifty years after independence, the spirit of the age has not triumphed, at least not to the extent to which Nehru had hoped. Despite some changes, much inequality still remains; and, along with it, the persistent rhetoric of equality. When one examines this rhetoric and the sources from which it comes—university vice-chancellors, judges of the higher courts, newspaper editors, and not just politicians and social activists—one may be excused for suspecting a certain lack of seriousness if not of sincerity in public discussions of equality.

The Hindu, 18 July 2001.

If there is anything distinctive about the Indian approach to equality, it is the continuous oscillation between the utopian and the fatalistic modes. The utopian mode is most in evidence in public presentations. At workshops, seminars and conferences where important social issues are discussed, one can always count on hearing stirring calls for an end to all inequalities, at least in the inaugural and valedictory sessions. There prominent persons in public life speak as if all the accumulated inequalities of the past can be made to tumble down like the walls of Jericho at the blast of the trumpets.

The opposite or fatalistic mode is characteristically expressed in private. There people are inclined to lament that nothing changes in India, or, if anything changes, the change is always for the worse. They point to the capitalist class, the bureaucracy, the elites and now, of course, the multinationals as the irremovable obstacles to the advance of equality. It is not as if the utopian and the fatalistic orientations are characteristic of two distinct and separate sets of persons. They coexist, like the two sides of a coin, in one and the same person.

The combined operation of the utopian and the fatalistic attitudes distorts our understanding of what is happening around us and obscures our view of the horizon of possibilities. Some forms of inequality are undoubtedly in decline while other forms of it are probably on the rise. Ours is a large, complex and changing society. So long as we continue to think of inequality as a single indivisible phenomenon that operates uniformly all across it, our understanding will remain clouded. There is no modern society in which inequalities are either rising or declining in every respect. Unless we discriminate between the major forms of inequality prevalent in our society—those inherited from the past and those of more recent growth—we will fail to discern any trends of change.

It is important to distinguish between the inequalities due to education, occupation and income from those due to caste and gender. The two types of inequality are no doubt intertwined in their operation, but they are different in their origin and in their legal and moral bases. One's caste and one's gender are unalterable. Where they are the main bases of inequality, the scope for changes in social position is severely restricted and the individual is encouraged to remain in the position ascribed at birth. The inequalities of caste were in principle transmitted from generation to generation. However large the inequalities due to occupation and education may be, the individual can always hope for a better social position, if not for himself, at least for his offspring.

Although they have not by any means disappeared, the inequalities due specifically to caste and gender are in decline and have been so for the last hundred years. The ritual idiom of purity and pollution through which they were expressed has weakened, though not to the same extent in all sectors of Indian society. The hierarchical conception of society which led men and women to accept their allotted positions in society as a part of the natural scheme of things has also weakened although it has not disappeared. All of this is obscured by the rhetoric of equality which has scant regard for secular, incremental changes.

New inequalities have arisen and extended their scope in Indian society in the last hundred years. The most important among these are the ones based on occupation and education. A new occupational system, quite different from anything that existed before the nineteenth century, has emerged in India. It is the basis of the modern Indian middle class as well as the organized working class. Along with the new occupational system there has emerged a new system of formal education. The educational system provides the credentials for entry into the new middle class including the higher levels of the occupational system.

. Modern economic systems are characterized by the continuous differentiation of occupations. There are tens of thousands of individual occupations. A major line of division is between manual and non-manual occupations. Manual occupations are divided into skilled, semi-skilled and unskilled ones. The non-manual occupations are legion, ranging from lowly clerical and other subordinate ones to superior professional, managerial and administrative ones. Thus, modern occupations are not only highly differentiated, they area also elaborately ranked. Occupational ranking is correlated, though not in any simple or straightforward way, with educational attainment and qualification.

Modern societies work through a variety of political, administrative, economic, financial, educational, scientific and other institutions. It is impossible to think of any such institution—a secretariat, a bank, a hospital, a laboratory or a university—without a set of graded occupations, manual as well as non-manual, enjoying unequal esteem, authority and income.

The social grading of occupations is a response to the demands of the institutions to which I have just referred. It is difficult to see how a bank can function if the manager and the peon are given equal authority, equal esteem and equal pay. The same holds by and large for a hospital, a laboratory or a university. If a university is to function effectively, the vice-chancellor must have more authority than the dean and he in turn more authority than the research assistant. This is not to say that anyone, the head of the institution included, should be invested with unlimited authority. The fact that authority in institutions is often abused cannot be an argument against the gradation of authority as such. Again, to say that in a hospital doctors are expected to receive greater esteem than laboratory attendants is not to suggest that the latter, or any category of hospital staff, may be treated with contempt.

Democratic societies of the present call for the equal consideration of all human beings as human beings, irrespective of race, caste and gender. But this does not mean that such societies can dispense with inequalities of authority, esteem and income in the institutions on which they depend for their sustenance.

Inequalities due to income, education and occupation cannot be eliminated, but they can be regulated. Regulating the inequalities of income may be difficult, but it is not beyond the reach of economic policy. Similarly, a great deal can be done to expand educational opportunities, although it will be difficult to provide education of the same quality to all members of society and impossible to ensure that they all achieve equal success in their educational careers. Again, while no social policy can eliminate the social ranking of occupations, it should be possible to provide a minimum of security and dignity to all positions, including the lowliest, within the occupational system. But the formulation of sensible policies for the regulation of inequality is obstructed by the rhetoric that all inequalities are dispensable and should be put to an end.

29

End of Inequality?

The Government of Madhya Pradesh has put in an advertisement in the *Economic and Political Weekly* (and presumably in other papers as well) declaring that it is 'Beginning to End Inequality'. Its aim is not the modest one of eliminating poverty, malnutrition and illiteracy or even of merely reducing inequality. It is the more ambitious one of putting an end, hopefully once and for all, to inequality itself. Such an aim may be appropriate to a messianic religious cult, but it is difficult to see how the Government of Madhya Pradesh, or any government, can bring inequality to an end. Messianic zeal in a secular government can lead to unforeseen, not to say unfortunate, consequences.

It is difficult to know what, apart from a diffuse feeling of benevolence, the authorities might have in their hearts and minds when they embark on a mission to end inequality. There are many different forms of inequality, and it would be unreasonable to expect all of them to be brought to an end immediately or simultaneously. Some forms of it, such as the practice of untouchability or bonded labour, are odious and reprehensible beyond any question. But these practices have already been abolished by law. If all that the Government of Madhya Pradesh is saying is that it will strive more diligently

The Telegraph, 28 December 2002.

to ensure that the laws are not violated with impunity, it is difficult to see why it should make such a dramatic declaration of intent.

Inequalities based on caste and gender are widespread in Indian society although more and more members of the educated middle class feel uneasy about them, whether or not they themselves are women or belong to castes hitherto regarded as inferior. In the past, inequalities of caste and gender were taken for granted and even regarded as a part of the natural scheme of things. Today the law is against discrimination on grounds of caste and gender, and public opinion is also turning against it although such opinion may not have a very wide reach. To the extent that any government is attempting to rally public opinion against the forms of invidious discrimination inherited from the past, its efforts must be endorsed.

Before embarking on a mission to bring inequality to an end, it may be useful to take stock of the way in which our society works and has been working for the last fifty to fifty-five years. Its operation is not governed wholly or even mainly by legislative and executive enactments. The history of India since independence has shown that it is easy enough to replace bad laws by good ones, but extremely difficult to change immemorial customs. Before independence we blamed the British for making bad laws or not making enough good ones. After independence we set about making good laws with a vengeance, but the social effects of those laws have been at best mixed. Our laws are now based on the premise of equality, but the bias of custom still remains largely in favour of hierarchy.

It is far from my intention to propose a fatalistic response to the obduracy of social custom; at the same time, we should not take recourse to utopian fantasies. Social customs relating to both caste and gender have in fact been changing, though very unevenly, in the last fifty years. The change is very marked in the metropolitan middle class, but almost imperceptible in remote rural communities. The loosening of customs has come about mainly through changes in education and employment. Populist politics has been more often a hindrance than a help in this process of change.

I am convinced that the long-term trend of change in Indian society is towards the weakening (though not the disappearance) of discrimination based on caste and gender. I believe further that the time is now ripe for organizing public opinion against such discrimination. But the weakening—or even the disappearance—of inequalities based on caste and gender will not bring all inequalities to an end. The very processes through which traditional forms of discrimination based on caste and gender are weakened create their own forms of inequality. What I have particularly in mind are the inequalities generated by a competitive educational and occupational system.

We cannot create a dynamic and competitive economy and at the same time bring all inequality to an end. Even if the competition is open and fair, there can at best be equality before the competition but not after it. The outcome of competition, whether in education or in employment, is not equality but inequality. That inequality is no doubt different from the one that is fixed at birth by race, caste or gender, but it is inequality all the same. It can no doubt be regulated by placing limits on the rewards of success and the penalties of failure. Such regulation has its limits and, when pushed beyond those limits, it brings development to a halt without leading to any significant reduction of inequality.

It is difficult to see how a modern university or hospital or bank can be run if all inequalities of income, esteem and authority among its members are levelled out. A policy of levelling was tried out in the Soviet Union in the aftermath of the Bolshevik Revolution. It was known as *uravnilovka*. Stalin realized that it would not work when he found that the engineers were dragging their feet because sufficient disparities were not being maintained between them and ordinary manual workers. Being a practical man and no mere ideological visionary, he soon denounced *uravnilovka* or levelling as a petty bourgeois fallacy. No one would accuse Stalin of being unaware of the dictum that all men are equal but some are more equal than others.

The problem with public institutions in India is not that there are ineluctable inequalities in them but that those inequalities take such crude and offensive forms. They offend not only our moral but also our aesthetic sensibilities. While some inequalities of income, esteem and authority are required for the operation of all modern institutions, they are in India elaborated far beyond those requirements, and what is elaborated acquires a life of its own. The apparatus of governance itself outdoes all institutions in the creation and elaboration of superfluous and wasteful hierarchical distinctions. Here I am talking not only of the costly and extravagant lifestyles of ministers but also of the proliferation of ranks and their corresponding perquisites that run through the entire governmental hierarchy. The long-suffering citizen will naturally wonder whether all or any of this will be touched by the fanfare attendant on the beginning to end inequality.

It is perhaps in the nature of things that politicians should set goals for the nation that they know will not be realized and that are perhaps unrealizable. The striking thing in India is that the extravagant statements made by politicians about the need to end inequality are so widely echoed by our public intellectuals who are nothing if they are not self-consciously virtuous. These extravagant statements divert attention away from more modest objectives such as controlling poverty, hunger, malnutrition, ill-health and illiteracy, and eliminating the more egregious forms of hierarchical distinction that pervade our public institutions. But that perhaps is what they are meant to do.

30

Poverty and Inequality

Poverty and inequality are two different things. The relationship between them is ambiguous and unclear, and the scholarly discussion of it bristles with unresolved difficulties. In India there is understandable public concern over both poverty and inequality, accompanied by a common presumption about the equivalence of the two. This presumption is reinforced by the writings of many economists who are inclined to treat poverty and inequality as the same thing, or more or less the same thing. The justified attack on poverty is quickly and effortlessly turned into an attack on inequality which is not always justified.

Rapid economic growth may lead to the simultaneous increase of both poverty and inequality. This is probably what happened in the early stages of industrialization in the West. The rigours of poverty and inequality in nineteenth-century England were described in vivid detail by writers as different from each other as Karl Marx and Charles Dickens. But it is difficult to be categorical. For if we take a long view of nineteenth-century England, we will find that even while economic inequality (or the inequality of income) was increasing, there was a slow but steady advance of legal equality and political equality. The advance of legal and political equality made it possible in course of time to attack the problem of poverty and to mitigate its rigours even while allowing some room for the growth of economic inequality.

The facts described above are well known to our economists, but they are easily overlooked by the self-righteous among them when they switch their attack from poverty to inequality. They seem to feel that the attack on inequality can be given greater strength and urgency if it is represented as being at the root of poverty. I am not saying that what happened in England in the nineteenth century must happen again and in the same way in India now. But we must learn from the experiences of others as well as our own experience in making clear conceptual distinctions.

Poverty is difficult to measure, and the measures are difficult to compare across space and over time. When the first results of systematic studies began to be published thirty years ago, they were almost immediately contested. There were disagreements among experts about data, concepts and methods. It is evident in retrospect that the early studies of poverty were not based on very secure empirical or theoretical foundations. Yet people quickly took positions on the basis of their findings. Scholars do not yield their ground readily unless the evidence against their position is overwhelming. Such evidence against an entrenched position takes years or even decades to accumulate. It would appear that the time has now come for a change of perspective on the issue of poverty in contemporary India.

It is well known that the estimates of poverty presented by Dandekar and Rath were criticized as being too high by two very eminent experts, V.K.R.V. Rao and P.V. Sukhatme. My impression is that in the 1970s and 1980s those who said that poverty was high and on the rise got a better hearing than their opponents. This was dictated as much by ideological as by scientific considerations. After thirty years of accumulated research, there is less room for disagreement now about how much poverty there is and whether it is increasing or decreasing.

It is enormously more difficult to arrive at agreed conclusions about inequality than about poverty. This means that arguments about inequality, its extent and direction of change, are even more vulnerable to ideological currents and counter-currents. There are many different forms and dimensions of inequality, and they do not all change at the same rate or even in the same direction. As I have already indicated, the advance of legal and political equality is often accompanied by an increase of economic inequality. Inequality has so many different aspects that it will be safe to say that, no matter what happens, one can find evidence of some increase in some aspect of it.

When people discuss poverty and inequality together, what they have in mind most commonly is economic inequality, or inequality of income and expenditure. This is largely because such inequality is relatively easy to measure. But it cannot be too strongly emphasized that income inequality is neither the only form of inequality nor the most important form of it. Many would say that inequality in the distribution of power or even the inequality of esteem and disesteem associated with social positions is more basic and fundamental. To presume that inequality is increasing overall simply because the Gini coefficient or some other measure of the distribution of income (or expenditure) has increased by a few decimal points would be a serious mistake.

Trends of change in inequality are much more difficult to read than those relating to poverty. The Constitution of India created a new framework of legal and political equality. The disabilities from which women and untouchables had suffered since time immemorial were rendered legally invalid by it. Many forms of social exclusion have been gradually relaxed if not eliminated. Many of the symbols of status through which traditional hierarchical distinctions were maintained have been rendered obsolete by the new educational and occupational systems. But all of this has not led to the elimination of inequalities in the distribution of life chances. The removal of disabilities is one thing, and the equalization of life chances another. An expanding economy cannot dispense with competition, and competition creates its own inequalities.

It is quite possible that there has been some increase of inequality in the distribution of income between regions and between rural and urban populations in some if not many parts of the country. Small fluctuations in the distribution of income between households are not always easy to detect or interpret. The data do not reveal a clear or consistent trend of increase (or decrease) of inequality in all regions and all sectors during the last fifty years. They certainly do not give support to the view that the rich are getting richer and the poor are getting poorer in the country as a whole. The rich are probably getting richer but the poor are also doing a little better, on the whole and in the aggregate.

No matter how strongly one might feel about the continuance of economic inequality, it has now become difficult to ignore the weight of the evidence which shows that there has been in the last fifteen years a clear decrease of households below the poverty line. There has been a decrease not only in the percentage of such households but also in their absolute number. There are disagreements about the extent of decline, and some feel that the rate of decline has slowed down and will slow down further. To be sure, there is nothing to be complacent about since the number of households below the poverty line is still enormous. But that should not lead us to disregard the record and say that poverty must be increasing since economic inequality is increasing.

In conclusion, the moral argument against poverty is altogether different from the moral argument against economic inequality. The kind of poverty that makes children go hungry and women die of malnutrition cannot be supported by any moral argument whatsoever. The case is altogether different with increases in the inequality of income between, say, corporate managers and higher civil servants or between civil servants and college teachers. Salary differentials within the middle class are at best matters of practical policy; they are not matters of conscience. Yet there are people who argue as if doomsday is near at hand when they confront evidence of such increase. This makes me wonder whether Justice Oliver Wendell Holmes was not right when he said, 'I have no respect for the passion for equality, which seems to me merely idealizing envy.' I will only add that the passion is often a simulated one since the social practice of many of the champions of equality is permeated by the most gross, flagrant and egregious forms of inequality.

31

The Working Class

The working class has received continuous attention from social and political commentators for well over a hundred years. Yet even in the middle of the nineteenth century, it was a new expression which brought into focus a new reality created by industrial capitalism, first in England and other Western countries, and then elsewhere. Until that time, it was common to speak about labourers but not about a working class. Before the advent of industrial capitalism, Western society was represented in terms of its division into estates just as Indian society was represented in terms of its division into varnas and jatis rather than of classes.

The classic formulation of the conditions of the working class may be found in the descriptive and analytical writings of Engels and Marx. Engels provided vivid descriptions of working class men, women and children in mid-nineteenth-century England while Marx developed a theory which maintained that that class would be the principal agent of historical change. That theory has had a profound influence on intellectual and political currents throughout the world. In it the workers as the 'owners merely of labour-power' are contrasted sharply with the owners of capital or the bourgeoisie. The idea of a working class or proletariat deprived of everything

The Hindu, 29 April 2003.

except its capacity to merely labour appealed to the imaginations of many who were themselves somewhat better placed. Some came to believe that the working class was by its very suffering destined to lead humanity as a whole to a better future.

The polarization of bourgeoisie and proletariat became a central theme in theories and programmes of political change through the conflict of classes. But the polarization did not take the course predicted by the theory. As the nineteenth century passed into the twentieth, it began to be evident that the 'owners merely of labour-power' were a mixed bag, and the passage of time seemed to make them more and not less of a mixed bag. Social and political attitudes were shaped not only by the structure of property but also, and independently of it, by the occupational structure, and there the distinction between non-manual and manual occupations could not be seen as merely an aspect of the one between capitalists and workers.

The gap between the working class and the middle class continued to be present even where the latter consisted mainly of 'owners merely of labour-power'. An important sociological study made by David Lockwood nearly fifty years ago showed how clerks and manual workers in Britain differed from each other. They differed in their market situations, in their work situations and, above all, in their status situations. Even when they had similar incomes, they had different patterns of expenditure, different lifestyles and different aspirations for their children.

Differences between the lower levels of non-manual employees and the upper levels of manual workers have not been of the same magnitude or significance in all places or at all times. The general disesteem of manual work common among agrarian societies was accentuated in the Indian case by traditional attitudes towards purity and pollution. But attitudes towards manual work, or at least some forms of it, are changing even in India in part as a result of changes in the technology and organization of work.

At the time of independence, India had a small middle class and a small industrial working class. Both have expanded considerably, and their expansion has brought some sections of workers, particularly in the organized sector, closer to some sections of the middle class in their market situation, their work situation and their status situation. This has happened in many parts of the world and some sociologists have called it 'embourgeoisement' or the process of 'becoming bourgeois'. But it is not a simple one-way process. For while workers have adopted many middle-class social standards, clerks and other non-manual employees, including teachers and doctors, have adopted many trade-union practices developed first by the industrial working class.

The very processes that have brought some sections of manual workers closer to the middle class have carried them further away from the majority of manual workers in a variety of occupations in the unorganized sector. Here the pay is very low, there is hardly any job security and the conditions of work are often appalling. So great is the disparity between these workers and those who constitute the aristocracy of labour that one might well ask if it is at all reasonable to speak of all workers, or even all manual workers, as belonging to a single class. The irony is that political movements and parties continue to use the imagery of nineteenth-century capitalism to make demands in the name of the 'owners merely of labour-power' whose benefits go not to the worst-off but to the best-off sections of manual workers and also to many non-manual workers.

Fifty years ago in India the differences between manual

and non-manual workers were clear and distinct. The wages of manual workers were generally, if not invariably, lower than the salaries of employees in clerical and related occupations. Even more than in Victorian England, in the city of Calcutta where I grew up in the late 1940s and the early 1950s, manual work was considered 'rough' whereas non-manual employment, no matter how poorly paid, was 'respectable'. In the West, technological changes since the Second World War have rendered manual work less rough and unclean. Similar changes are taking place in India although they are as yet largely confined to the organized sector outside of which manual work continues to be onerous and disagreeable.

Differences between manual workers and clerical and other employees were not confined to the workplace. They were equally if not more marked in the home and the neighbourhood. In the city of Calcutta, and I presume in other Indian cities, clerks and manual workers lived in different neighbourhoods, although shortage of housing and unemployment were leading some downwardly mobile members of the middle class to move into slums. The reverse movement, of well-paid and upwardly mobile manual workers into middle-class neighbourhoods, was to begin later, and even now it is not much more than a trickle.

In addition to developments in the technology and organization of work, the spread of literacy and education has played a part in altering the balance between the higher grades of manual and the lower grades of non-manual employees. In nineteenth-century England, manual workers in factories had little or no education whereas the ability to read and write was essential for clerical and related occupations. It took factory workers more than one generation to recognize that even if they themselves had missed out on schooling, their children would benefit by being sent to school. As schooling becomes universal, the disparities between manual and non-manual workers are bound to become softened, although differences in the amount and quality of education still remain even in England which was the first industrial nation.

The equation between factory work and no education, and office work and some education held to a very large extent in India at the time of independence. It does not hold to the same extent any longer. It hardly needs to be repeated that the expansion of literacy and education was painfully slow in the decades immediately after independence, but things have begun to change. Many public sector undertakings now have their own schools which provide subsidized education to the children of workers. Sometimes this education is better than what is available to children whose parents are in lower white-collar employment in small establishments outside the public sector. Again, the vast masses of those who are in casual or unregulated employment find schooling of even the most elementary kind outside the reach of their children. Even when those children manage to get to school, they drop out before long and they reproduce the life histories of their parents. Such enormous and perhaps increasing disparities in life chances among workers in different occupations and in different sectors of the economy lead us back to the question as to what people really mean when they speak of the working class in contemporary India.

32

The Indian Middle Class

The Indian middle class has many critics, the most eloquent among them being almost without exception members of that class itself. Middle-class Indians tend to oscillate between self-congratulation and self-recrimination although the oscillation takes different forms in different sections of the class, such as academics, lawyers and civil servants.

I was recently saying to a civil servant of my acquaintance that, compared with officers of the defence forces, members of the Indian Administrative Service (IAS) seemed to be always running their service down. He did not disagree but added that the typical IAS officer attacked his service mainly in order to indicate that he himself was a total exception to the general pattern. It was in other words a form of self-congratulation at the expense of the institution he served. Of course no one can match the agility with which intellectuals in general, and left intellectuals in particular, direct praise to themselves while attacking the corrupt and obtuse middle class.

The Indian middle class deserves serious attention today if only because of its great size and diversity. It has grown steadily in size since independence and particularly in the last couple of decades. At a moderate estimate it will number

The Hindu, 5 February 2001.

over 100 million persons which is more than the total population of any European country, save Russia. The Indian middle class, like the middle class anywhere in the world, is differentiated in terms of occupation, education and income. But the peculiarity of the class in India is its diversity in terms of language, religion and caste. It is by any reckoning the most polymorphous middle class in the world. The problems of the contemporary middle class derive as much from this polymorphy as from its roots in India's colonial experience.

A new middle class began to emerge in India in the middle of the nineteenth century in the womb of an ancient hierarchical society. The society within which it began to take shape was not a society of classes, but of castes and communities. Even though it has grown enormously in size and importance in the last hundred and fifty years, its growth has not led to the disappearance of the multitudinous castes and communities inherited from the past. The peculiarity of the Indian middle class arises not so much from its intrinsic character as a class as from the social environment within which it has to operate.

The new middle class first emerged in the presidency capitals of Calcutta, Bombay and Madras in the law courts, the hospitals, the banks and the offices set up for commercial, administrative and other purposes. The backbone of the middle class is a particular kind of occupational system which was new in the nineteenth century, at least outside the West, but has now become a worldwide phenomenon. It is a highly differentiated system with clerical and other subordinate non-manual occupations at one end and superior professional, managerial and administrative ones at the other. These occupations enjoy unequal esteem and authority and are unequally paid; and it is possible that income inequalities between them are now rising.

Middle-class occupations are non-manual ones and require some measure of formal education. The growth of a new middle class is accompanied by the growth of a new educational system. Education has become institutionalized to an unprecedented extent, and more persons of both sexes spend more time in schools, colleges and universities than they ever did before. Educational institutions provide not only the skills but also the credentials required for entry into middle-class occupations. The expansion of education has been haphazard and uneven, and part of the reason for the debasement of the middle class is the debasement of education in the last fifty years.

There are deep inequalities within the middle class and between it and other social classes. Public-spirited Indians are justifiably concerned about these inequalities, particularly where they feel that they may be increasing rather than decreasing. Some part of the inequality arises from the very nature of the occupational and educational systems that define the middle class. But some of it is also a carry over from the traditional social order. Inequalities based on occupation, income and education are in principle different from the traditional ones based on caste and gender.

The middle-class orientation to inequality is competitive and not hierarchical as in the old social order. It must not be forgotten that a competitive system generates inequality even where the competition is fair, and in India it is not particularly fair. People use the advantages of family, kinship and caste to push ahead without much consideration for the cost to others or for the rules of the game. An expanding middle class has an ugly face and its members often appear as callous and self-serving to those who are attached to the traditional order in which individuals remained in the social positions assigned to them at birth.

In the old order the hierarchical relations between castes and between men and women were expressed in the ritual idiom of purity and pollution, perhaps the most compelling idiom devised by human ingenuity for keeping a social hierarchy in place. While the idiom of purity and pollution was all-pervasive, it bore most heavily on the weaker sections of society, notably untouchables and women. The preoccupation with pollution led to the permanent segregation of untouchables and the periodic segregation of women during their monthly courses; and the obsession with the purity of women, particularly among the upper castes, led to their being required to marry very young, preferably before the onset of puberty.

There has been a steady and continuous decline in practices associated with purity and pollution both in inter-caste relations and in the relations between men and women since the middle of the nineteenth century. The elaborate rules relating to inter-dining and food transactions between castes have become greatly attenuated. The practice of untouchability has also declined although it has been replaced to some extent by the practice of atrocities against untouchables. The segregation of women during their monthly periods is no longer observed as in the past, and there has been a secular trend of increase in their age at marriage. While these trends are visible everywhere, they are most clearly in evidence in the middle class, particularly among those in professional, administrative, and managerial occupations.

It can be easily demonstrated that the decline in the practices of purity and pollution by which the traditional social hierarchy was sustained has been directly associated with the social and cultural ascendance of the middle class. The plain fact is that those practices are inconsistent with the functional requirements of the modern occupational and educational systems and of modern institutions in general. A bank, a law court or a newspaper office cannot function effectively today if women employees have to be segregated during their periods and if large sections of the population have to be denied employment because their near or distant ancestors engaged in activities deemed to be ritually defiling. It may well be that in discrediting the cultural basis of the traditional hierarchy, the middle class has been acting in accordance with enlightened self-interest. We may not wish to give it too much credit for this, but we must understand and acknowledge the consequences of its ascendance. It has certainly not led to the elimination of inequality but it has rendered obsolete some of its most oppressive and odious forms.

The middle class has played the leading part in the modernization of Indian society; without it there would be no modernization. It is for this reason viewed with mistrust by two kinds of intellectuals: the traditional and the post-modern. The former mistrust the middle class because its ascendance cannot but undermine many elements of the traditional social order, including some beneficial ones. The latter are hostile to it because the middle class is directly and indirectly the heir of the Enlightenment which is gall and wormwood to post-modernism.

33

The Russian Intelligentsia

Russia has experienced major changes in its social, economic and political arrangements in the last hundred years. The Bolshevik Revolution created a momentous upheaval within Russia, and developments there directly affected many countries in the neighbourhood. The changes set in motion by Gorbachev and Yeltsin towards the close of the twentieth century appear to be no less momentous. What impact have these successive changes had on the class structure of Russia and of other east and central European countries? More specifically, what is the place of the intelligentsia in Russian society today?

The Russian intelligentsia created a place for itself in public life and became a recognized social category under the Tsarist regime. It consisted of writers and others who wrote and spoke on behalf of the submerged masses, and acted as the conscience of society. It set itself in opposition to the ruling class, although many of its members came from the fringes of that class. It was of course quite distinct from the peasantry and also from the workers who were emerging with the emergence of industry, although it espoused their cause against the established order.

The Bolshevik Revolution sought to wipe out the old social

The Telegraph, 10 June 2004.

order and its oppressive class structure. It was, in Lenin's phrase, a revolution of the peasants and workers under the leadership of the working class. As the socialist regime consolidated itself, workers and peasants became, at least in terms of numbers, the two most important components of society. Capitalists and landowners had been eliminated or marginalized with the abolition of private ownership of capital and land. But there was also another component of society, and it began to grow in size and strength. This was the intelligentsia.

Soviet society came to be represented in a distinct way under Stalin. This representation continued after his death, and it was also adopted by other east European regimes. In it society was shown as being divided into two classes, workers and peasants, and one stratum, the intelligentsia. Peasants and workers were generally described as classes, but sometimes all three components might be described as strata. The intelligentsia, on the other hand, was always described as a stratum and never as a class.

Soviet social theorists were formalists after a fashion. Workers and peasants constituted separate classes, not because they were engaged in different occupations but because they were related differently to the means of production. Workers worked in factories which were owned by the state whereas peasants worked on farms which were owned generally by collectives. Even after the abolition of private ownership of the means of production there still remained differences in the ownership of the means of production, hence differences of class. Actually most farms were collective farms or *kolkhozes*, but there were also state farms or *sovkhozes*, and those who cultivated the land on the latter were workers and not peasants.

Separate from the distinction according to association with

different forms of property was the distinction between manual and mental work. Soviet theory took a very distinctive view of mental or non-manual workers. Whether as administrators, managers, engineers, scientists or doctors, they were members of a stratum, the intelligentsia. They were quite different from their counterparts in capitalist society who belonged to the middle class. There was no middle class in socialist society because there was no private ownership of the means of production, and because employees of the state, whether in manual or non-manual occupations, did not work for private gain.

If in the Soviet Union manual and non-manual workers were both by and large employed in state undertakings, why was a distinction maintained between the workers and the intelligentsia? Why were they not both designated simply as workers? I believe that this was a concession to the reality of occupational differentiation in a rapidly developing economy, although it was given a distinctive ideological colouring. Marx may have subordinated occupational differentiation to the divisions of property, but the occupational structure of industrial societies had changed substantially since his time. Scientists and engineers differed in many important ways from turners and fitters, but they too were important for the development of the Soviet economy.

The makers of the Soviet system had inherited the dogma that the ultimate creator of value was labour, meaning mainly manual work. That dogma made it very difficult to incorporate into the working class people who did not work with their hands. At the same time, scientists, engineers, diplomats, administrators and pen-pushers of a lower order were also needed in the service of the state and the people. The category of the intelligentsia was sufficiently elastic to accommodate mental workers of every conceivable kind. But the intelligentsia had to be a stratum and not a class, for to represent them as a class might awaken misgivings about conflicts of interest between it and the working class. Peasants and workers could be described as classes because their spheres of action were too far apart for such misgivings to arise in a serious way.

What of the present? My understanding is that in Russia and other east European countries people now talk less and less about the intelligentsia, even as a stratum, than they did in the past. The social structure has changed, and the tone of public discussion has also changed. Many new forms of non-manual employment have emerged. The concept of the intelligentsia might be stretched to accommodate the commissar, but hardly the owner of a small business. Moreover, the old inhibition against talking about the middle class has largely been laid to rest. Russians are now free to talk not only of the middle class but also of the 'oligarchs' who bring to mind the robber barons who played such a notable part in the building of capitalism in America.

It is interesting how the idea of the intelligentsia as a distinct social category became established in a particular part of the world. It did not acquire currency in western Europe or North America where the idea of the intellectual carries a very different connotation from that of the intelligentsia as understood in eastern Europe. It would now appear that the use of the idea was limited not only to a particular geographical area but also to a particular historical phase. In India, the late Ashok Rudra sought to employ the concept in his analysis of economic and political dominance. But he saw the intelligentsia as a class, in alliance with capitalists and landowners, which, of course, is contrary to the Soviet conception of it as a stratum with no sectional interest of its own.

Russian society is undergoing a process of churning. What

is more, there is no organ of state or society that can provide a representation of it, such as the one according to which it was divided into two classes and one stratum, that will be generally considered as authoritative. One can talk freely now about inequalities and conflicts of interest, and one need not push oneself too hard to distinguish between a class and a stratum. But a clear and coherent picture of the changing social order in Russia awaits the emergence of a new generation of social theorists whose task will have to be different from that of its immediate predecessors.

34

Normative Convergence

The working class and the middle class have both been subjects of considerable interest to sociologists, economic historians and political analysts. They emerged together with the emergence of industrial capitalism, first in the West and then in other parts of the world. Each country has its distinctive pattern of classes. The American working class is not the same as the French, not to speak of the Indian one, and this holds true also of the middle class. At the same time, there are family resemblances among the varieties of each of the two major classes wherever they exist.

Socialists have always taken an interest in the working class and to some extent also in the middle class, particularly in its relationship with the former. The socialist movement itself may be viewed as a movement for the advancement of the working class initiated largely by the middle class. This movement has contributed something to the changes in the character of both the classes, although the changes that have actually taken place have been different from what was anticipated.

Among Marxists it was long believed that the main distinction among classes was the one between the owners and the non-owners of the means of production, or between capitalists and workers. But another distinction has turned

Not previously published.

out to be at least as important, and that is the distinction between manual and non-manual, or blue- and white-collar, employees. The differentiation of occupations has acquired a significance and complexity that was not foreseen in the nineteenth century. This is a worldwide phenomenon although developments have differed from one country to another, depending upon technology, economic organization and political regime.

Today when people think of the distinction between the middle class and the working class, they think mainly of the distinction between manual and non-manual occupations. This distinction is not equally marked in all societies. Oddly enough, it was more marked in the Soviet Union when it had a socialist regime than in the United States under a capitalist one. A section of society bearing many similarities with the middle class in Western societies emerged in the Soviet Union, only it was called the intelligentsia and characterized not as a class but as a stratum. Today of course the presence of a middle class is acknowledged in Russia, and there are many continuities between that class and the stratum known earlier as the intelligentsia.

The distinction between the middle class and the working class is not merely economic, it is also social and cultural. It is, as I have just indicated, more marked in some countries than in others, it being particularly well marked in India. Students of class in both Britain and the United States have noted that the social and cultural distinctions between the two classes have become progressively muted during the last five or six decades. The question is: are there indications of something similar now happening in India?

Changes in technology, market conditions and legal provisions have steadily altered the nature of manual work and the status of manual workers in the advanced industrial societies and beyond. Manual work is not necessarily as onerous or irksome or unpleasant as it generally was a hundred years ago. No less important is the fact that elementary education has become universal in many countries and is becoming so in many others. This means that manual workers are no longer largely unlettered as they were in the past. With changes in the conditions of work and life, changes have come about in the social attitudes and values of the working class.

The material conditions of industrial workers began to improve after the Second World War. Sociologists in Britain and America noted that those who did well were increasingly adopting middle-class aspirations and middle-class attitudes to work and home. A similar process may now be seen at work in India albeit on a very restricted canvas. Since the 1950s Western sociologists have described this process as 'embourgeoisement' or becoming bourgeois.

There has undoubtedly been the adoption by some sections of workers of cultural attitudes and values characteristic of the middle class, but this has not been a one-way process. Sections of the middle class have increasingly adopted political values and attitudes that were in the past distinctive of the working class. It is this two-way process to which the term 'normative convergence' may be applied. Here it must be stressed that there is at best a tendency towards convergence; this tendency is unlikely to level out all distinctions on the plane of values between the middle class and the working class even in the West, not to speak of India.

What are typical middle-class values? In what ways are they different from typical working-class values? It is impossible to answer these questions in a short space because there is much variation and a great deal of change in both middle- and working-class values. Certain contrasts have however been noted since the middle of the nineteenth century when these classes began to acquire shape in the first industrial country, Britain. A consideration of these contrasts will throw light on developments in contemporary India.

The middle class has always placed a high value on individual achievement through success in education and employment. It has traditionally looked to advancement through individual mobility rather than collective action. Collective action for economic and social advantage has been the characteristic strategy of the working class. The trade-union movement was essentially a movement of workers, no matter which class might provide it with leadership.

Socialization in the family and neighbourhood differed between the middle and the working class. The middle-class family was more self-contained and more private than the working-class one, and gave more attention to success at school for its children. If these were once distinctively middle-class orientations, they are no longer exclusively so. After the War a class of affluent workers began to emerge in Britain and other Western countries whose members were better paid and better educated; and they were increasingly motivated to follow the paths to individual success already being followed by clerks and other subordinate non-manual employees. The attitudes and values of these workers were perceptibly different from those common among miners, dockers, railwaymen and other sections of the old working class.

The adoption of middle-class living standards and middle-class aspirations regarding individual mobility through education and employment is now beginning to be noted in India among workers in the organized sector. Particularly in the larger public sector enterprises, where housing and schooling are made available by the company, children from a mix of classes develop common attitudes and common aspirations. Where such companies favour children of their employees in the selection for jobs and where a manual worker's son does well at school, he can look forward to white-collar employment in course of time.

Because manual workers develop aspirations for upward mobility through education and employment for themselves or their children, it does not follow that they give up the pursuit of material advancement through collective action. In fact, that pursuit may be continued with greater vigour. What is more important is that material advancement through collective action has now become an accepted part of middle-class culture. In India, not only has white-collar trade unionism gained widespread, not to say universal, acceptance, but aggressive, even militant trade unionism by higher professionals such as professors, doctors and lawyers has become a matter of routine.

As a university teacher in India, I witnessed a sea-change in the professional culture of academics in the last four or five decades. Joint industrial action by the unions of academic and non-academic staff exemplifies normative convergence in a concrete form. Prolonged strikes and noisy demonstrations are taken for granted by both teachers and students in universities just as they are by both doctors and patients in hospitals. One has only to think back on professors and doctors at the time of independence to recognize the change in the propensity for collective action. The working class is learning a few things from the middle class, but so is the middle class from the workers.

VI
Discrimination and Reservation

Discrimination is still widely practised in Indian society. Caste continues to be perhaps the most important basis of social discrimination, but it is also practised on the basis of religion, language and class.

It has often been said that traditional Indian society was remarkably tolerant of diversity. But its tolerance included the tolerance of untouchability and the perpetual tutelage of women. Caste-based discrimination, particularly against the Dalits, is still widely in evidence despite strong constitutional and legal provisions against it.

India's democratic legal and political order has sought to redress the inequalities inherited from the past. The programme of positive discrimination in favour of the Backward Classes is among the oldest and most extensive of such programmes in the world. The scope of the Indian programme is so vast that it would be unrealistic to expect uniform results from it. Positive discrimination has led to a somewhat better representation of disadvantaged castes and communities in public employment, and it has contributed to the creation of a middle class among the Scheduled Castes and Tribes. But it has also led to a strengthening of identity politics, and sometimes to the view that in public institutions representation matters more than the maintenance of standards. Affirmative action, properly applied, has a positive contribution to make to social change, but in India it is rendered counterproductive where it is reduced simply to a system of numerical quotas.

35

Tolerance and Exclusion

Indian society is marked by two contradictory features: the wide tolerance of diverse beliefs, faiths and ways of life, and the stringent observance of social exclusion. This has been the case for a very long time although the balance between tolerance and exclusion has not always been the same.

Those who are inclined to present a positive view of the Indian social tradition stress the tolerance of diversity and argue that India's pluralist culture gives it a natural advantage in the pursuit of democracy. Of course they can see the tides of communal intolerance sweeping through the country, but these they regard as aberrations whose origins they attribute to external forces. It is in a way natural not to look too closely at the contradictions lodged in one's own society but instead to blame others for its maladies. Secular and left-oriented intellectuals tend to attribute most if not all the social and political maladies of contemporary India to the colonial regime and to some extent the ones which came after it on independence. Other nationalists go a little further and attribute them not just to British rule but even more to Muslim rule which preceded it. Left- and right-wing intellectuals have this in common that they both assign the responsibility for the breakdown of order, harmony and unity to some external

The Hindu, 6 March 2003.

agency—the British imperialists in one case, and a combination of British imperialists and Muslim invaders in the other.

On the opposite side are those who point to the myriad forms of social exclusion prevalent in India from ancient to modern times. This was the case with many civil servants and missionaries in colonial times who dwelt with relish on the Indian's preoccupation with exclusion and segregation in the past as well as the present.

No one can deny the profusion of languages, styles of life and religious beliefs and practices that have coexisted in India since time immemorial. The makers of modern India—Tagore, Gandhi and Nehru—took pride in the tolerance of diversity which they regarded as the defining feature of India's civilization and the most valuable part of its cultural heritage.

The linguistic diversity of India is truly astonishing. Languages belonging to the Indo-Aryan and Dravidian families have coexisted—and flourished—for hundreds of years. Sanskrit was introduced into the south many centuries ago, and it influenced the ritual idiom as well as the everyday language of the people; but it did not by any means extinguish the great Dravidian languages. The British introduced the English language into India, and its use has become more and not less widespread since independence: some of the best writers in the English language in the world today—Salman Rushdie, Vikram Seth and Amitav Ghosh—are Indians or of Indian origin. Again, the spread of English through the length and breadth of the country has not led to the death or decay of any of the major Indian languages.

Most of the major religions of the world are to be found in India. Some of them, such as Hinduism and Buddhism, originated in the land while others, such as Christianity and Islam, which came from outside, have remained and grown in it for a thousand years and more. Islam did not bring

Hinduism to an end, and Hinduism did not drive out Christianity. Each of the major religions is divided into a variety of sects and denominations. This great profusion of linguistic, religious and other customs and usages was associated with a multitude of castes and communities each of which was the bearer of a particular sub-culture or even sub-sub-culture which it transmitted from generation to generation.

The coexistence of the multitude of castes and communities with their diverse cultural practices was in the best of times maintained by a complicated balance of accommodation and exclusion. It cannot be too strongly emphasized that cultural diversity was always accompanied by a measure of social separation. Social separation was the general principle and social exclusion, as in the case of the untouchables and other marginalized or stigmatized groups, was only the extreme form taken by it. Separation and exclusion were established features of the social structure well before the British or even the Muslims came to India.

Separation and exclusion were maintained through the rules of commensality and connubium which regulated the exchange of food (roti) and of brides or daughters (beti). Only those belonging to the same community could freely exchange food and daughters; beyond that, there were restrictions of many different kinds. For all the damage that colonial rule may have done to the pride and self-respect of educated Indians, it did not invent either *roti vyavahar* or *beti vyavahar*.

Social separation and social exclusion were not unknown elsewhere, but the rules regulating food transactions were unusually elaborate, and those regulating marriage transactions unusually stringent in India. They did not preclude social interaction, even close and amicable interaction, between communities, but gave such interaction a distinctive character. Restrictions relating to food have become greatly attenuated as a result of modernization, to the point where many of them appear absurd even to those who remain very conscious of their caste or communal identity. Restrictions relating to marriage have also eased, but not nearly to the same extent, and marriage within the caste or community is still the general practice.

Restrictions on food and marriage transactions were often, though not always, governed by considerations of superior and inferior rank and status. A group deemed superior might accept daughters from groups deemed inferior but would not give its own daughters in marriage to them: this is the principle of hypergamy or anuloma, discussed at some length in the classical literature. In the matter of food, it was the other way around. A group deemed superior might not accept food, or at least cooked food, or food cooked in water from one deemed inferior, but the latter might accept any kind of food from the former. In these cases, division went along with hierarchy. Today, under the influence of democratic politics, the sense of hierarchy has become weakened, but the sense of division remains and may in some cases have even become strengthened. In India, as elsewhere, democratic politics has had many unforeseen consequences.

As already indicated, separation sometimes took the extreme form of exclusion from the basic amenities of social life. There might be separation between two sub-castes of Brahmins, for instance, the Smartha and Shri Vaishnava Brahmins of Tamil Nadu, in regard to both food and marriage transactions. Very different from that was the separation imposed on what were known as the exterior castes. Again, it has to be emphasized that the accommodation of diversity did not necessarily entail either equality or reciprocity. The system worked reasonably well and maintained a certain stability so long as each caste and community more or less knew and accepted its place in the general scheme of things. Democracy has destabilized the traditional hierarchy, and there is no way of putting it back in place again. It hardly helps to say that there was democracy of a certain kind in the past—village democracy or some other kind of democracy—and that we can try to go back to it. There simply is no going back to the past.

Centuries of separation and exclusion have led each caste and community to develop a strong sense of its collective identity and collective interest. The normal tendency of economic development is to blur the traditional boundaries between communities, but economic development in the last fifty years has had that effect to only a limited extent. Democratic politics has, if anything, heightened the suspicion and mistrust between communities. Memories of exclusion, suffered for generations, are easily revived and they set caste against caste and community against community. The backward communities and the minorities feel that they are getting too little while the others feel that they are asking for too much. The accommodation of diversity is a very different thing in a democratic society from what it was in a hierarchical one.

36

Coping with Caste Discrimination

Dalit activists and human rights gurus have joined hands to press for the inclusion of caste discrimination and the practice of untouchability on the agenda of the UN conference at Durban on racism and racial discrimination. This is wrong because caste is not a form of race and untouchability, no matter how reprehensible, is not a form of racial discrimination. The Government of India is determined to prevent this, presumably because it does not want its dirty linen to be aired outside. This is futile because in a democracy there is no effective way of preventing the discussion outside the country of social evils that are known to exist within it.

There is no harm in discussing, whether inside or outside India, the discriminatory practices of caste, including untouchability, and I have done so myself in papers and articles published in India and abroad. But the discussion should be in good faith and not under false pretences. Some of those who wish to include caste discrimination in the agenda at Durban know very well that caste is not a form of race, but they are not averse to stretching the point somewhat in the service of a good cause.

One must not misuse the metaphor of race even in a good cause and who will deny that the abolition of untouchability

The Times of India, 30 August 2001.

is a good cause? Extensive misuse of the metaphor of race has had tragic consequences in Europe. Once it is conceded that caste discrimination is a form of racial discrimination, there will be nothing to prevent religious or linguistic minorities from saying that they too are victims of racial discrimination. It is well to remember what the noted geneticist and biometrician J.B.S. Haldane had said: 'As for the word race, it has so many different meanings as to be useless in scientific discussion, though very useful for getting members of the same nation to hate one another.'

I am convinced that the Government of India is not in favour of caste discrimination or the practice of untouchability. They are not in its own interest. To represent the government as being opposed, or even indifferent, to the abolition of untouchability is to act in bad faith, whether one does it in Delhi or in Durban.

I do not wish to suggest that the Government of India itself acts in good faith in all matters, because it does not. Its basic instinct is to brush all unpleasant things under the carpet, and to filter out every hint of dissent: no arguments please, we are all Indians. Bureaucracy can be particularly obdurate. Some thirty years ago I was briefly involved, along with the late Professor V.M. Dandekar, in a project sponsored by a UN agency to study the economic and social implications of the Green Revolution. The project required clearance from two ministries of the Government of India. At the first meeting there were two joint secretaries who told us they had no objection to the economic side of the project because India was doing well economically but that they were worried about the social side since it was bound to deal with caste and other practices which would show India in a bad light. I was appalled. But I need not have worried, because Professor

Dandekar, who did not suffer fools gladly, wiped the floor with the two joint secretaries.

It is the same obstructive mindset that leads the government to issue fatwas from time to time to restrict the entry of foreign scholars into India or their participation in seminars and conferences. I am not talking now about restrictions imposed on particular individuals whose bonafides may be in question, but a blanket ban on foreign scholars on the ground that they may hear or say things that could damage India's reputation abroad. This is bizarre for the simple reason that Indian academics are in general better equipped than Indian bureaucrats to deal with foreign critics of India; and they are no less patriotic.

The government has been caught on the wrong foot by a combination of elements that seems to have no hesitation in embarrassing it. When it comes to media attention, the NGOs can beat the government hands down, nationally as well as internationally. The NGO explosion is a phenomenon of the last ten or fifteen years, and nobody really understands how the NGOs have grown or what role they will play in the society of the future. At one level one can say that they have expanded in response to the failure of the government on the social front, just as the market has expanded in response to its failures on the economic front.

The ascendancy of the NGOs, like the ascendancy of the market, is a worldwide phenomenon, driven in some respects by the same forces. The NGOs are not only a worldwide phenomenon, there is a strong international presence in them though this may be less visible in India than in smaller countries such as Nepal, Bangladesh and Sri Lanka. Again, this is not necessarily a bad thing, and, certainly, in a large and self-confident country such as ours there is no need to be paranoid about it. Any attempt by the government to come down with a heavy hand on the NGOs collectively will be counterproductive, and it will backfire.

At the same time, there must be wider public scrutiny of what the NGOs are actually doing. The getting together of Dalit activists and human rights gurus may have a lesson to offer, but it is doubtful that the Government of India will learn it. Such an alliance might not have been possible or effective without the abundant presence of NGOs ready to take on the government in the cause of social justice. The activists provide the youth, the energy and the dynamism, and the gurus the wisdom often gathered in the corridors of power in national and international agencies.

Personally speaking, I have some sympathy for the Dalit activists even when I find their approach wrong-headed. Their movement is driven by a genuine passion to break free from a monstrously oppressive social system. I cannot say the same for the human rights gurus. Their social and occupational background is very different. They are usually much older persons often with successful careers in the civil service, in diplomacy or in the judiciary behind them. I do not envy them their frequent visits abroad at public expense. What I deeply regret is that there is so little of intellectual worth in what they say or write about the creation of a more just and humane society. And as to their passion, it is often a simulated passion.

37

Discrimination at Work

Discrimination in matters relating to work is a cause for growing concern all over the world. The International Labour Organization has sought to prohibit it through the adoption of a set of Core Labour Standards. While unexceptionable in themselves, these standards are not always easy to apply in all parts of the world, and they become a source of friction between national and international agencies. National governments do their best to resist scrutiny by outside bodies while international agencies tend to adopt a self-consciously virtuous attitude towards problems that are complex, not to say intractable.

Discrimination, at work and outside work, is widespread in Indian society. Indeed, discrimination on the basis of caste and gender was the rule rather than the exception in India's traditional hierarchical order. In the past the entire division of labour was caste based and gender based. Even though discrimination is now forbidden by the new constitution and the new laws, many of the old practices, being deeply rooted in the habits of the past, continue to operate. This does not mean that there has been no change in attitudes and values among Indians. This change, however, has not been uniform, much depending on the nature of work and on its institutional setting.

The Hindu, 11 July 2002.

Without denying the great harm done to economic and social life by the more odious forms of discrimination, one must be careful not to tar all forms of it with the same brush. For many persons working with international agencies and for NGOs, the very word 'discrimination' acts like a red rag to the bull, and such persons often lack the patience and the inclination to distinguish between the practice of discrimination and allegations or suspicions of it. Well-intentioned but ill-judged attacks against discrimination in no matter what form or context can lead to avoidable confusion and needless acrimony.

The Indian experience shows how difficult it is to define, to detect and to regulate discrimination at work. Nothing can be more misconceived than the belief that every form of discrimination is invidious discrimination. Discrimination at work that arises from differences of ability and performance is not invidious discrimination. It is in conformity with the law, not only in India but in every modern society, and without it educational, technological and economic advancement would be impossible. Yet those who are hurt by it are inclined to believe that it is, particularly when they belong to sections of society whose members have in fact been regular victims of invidious discrimination.

It is difficult to see how a modern educational system or a modern occupational system could work without a system of rewards and penalties based on ability and performance. It may well be desirable to place social limits on the rewards of success as well as on the penalties of failure. But to award rewards and penalties to all alike, whether in a school, an office or a factory, without consideration of ability or performance would be both inefficient and unjust.

In India the law is against invidious discrimination based on race, caste and gender, but it does not regard all discrimination as invidious or harmful. It has in fact extensive provisions for benign or positive discrimination in favour of socially disadvantaged groups such as the Scheduled Tribes, the Scheduled Castes and the Other Backward Classes. These provisions have been in operation for several decades. They have done some good but have also created resentment. Upper-caste men who have been denied appointment or promotion because of rules favouring the weaker sections of society feel that the rules themselves are unjust and politically motivated, and that they devalue ability and performance. Lower-caste men and women feel that appointment or promotion does not protect them from informal and insidious discrimination practised against them both in and outside work by their superiors, their peers and even their subordinates.

Discrimination at work takes many different forms in India because work itself is organized differently from one setting to another. Only a small part of the workforce is deployed in the 'organized' sector. Outside that sector it is difficult to regulate discrimination, or indeed the conditions of work in general, through legislation. In much of the 'informal' sector workers are complicit in violations of the law either because they are unaware of the provisions of the law or because their livelihood depends on such violations. Here invidious discrimination is so widespread as to be taken for granted by both employers and employees.

In the traditional economic order, in the farm and the cottage, discrimination on the basis of caste and gender was in conformity with social norms and not against them. Men and women, and members of different castes were treated not only differently but also unequally. But that does not mean that those who were viewed as socially inferior could be oppressed and abused without any regard for custom or morality. It should not be forgotten that hierarchical societies have their own codes of conduct, however different those might be from the codes acceptable in democratic societies. The sanctions of the family and the community protected individuals from the abuse of discriminatory rules. Traditional sanctions have become greatly attenuated and the new ones are as yet weak and ineffectual.

A great deal of work in the informal sector today is outside the reach of the law and it is also detached from the sanctions of the family and the community. Here the problem is not so much with the definition or even the detection of discrimination as with its regulation. Discrimination is open and bare-faced, and in violation of both law and custom. The practice of invidious discrimination here is but a part of the larger practice of illegal and extra-legal activities.

We have to distinguish, first, between legitimate and illegitimate forms of discrimination, and, second, between mild and severe forms of it. Discrimination on grounds of caste and gender, no matter how mild, is illegitimate in the modern workplace. This is not to say that mild forms of invidious discrimination at work are easy to detect or to regulate in India or anywhere. They are in fact endemic in many parts of the world. But the point to bear in mind is that in the organized sector in India there are sanctions against them and mechanisms for their redress, even though the sanctions and the mechanisms are by no means foolproof.

While it is easy enough to distinguish in principle between discrimination based on caste and gender and that based on ability and performance, it is extremely difficult to do so in practice. The American experience has shown how easy it is to represent discrimination that is at bottom based on race prejudice or gender bias as being based on ability and performance. Where there are legal sanctions against invidious discrimination, the practice of it has to be established case by case. It is by no means easy to establish in each case whether the complainant suffered because of belonging to a disesteemed group or because of poor ability and performance.

It hardly needs to be repeated that gender and caste prejudices are widespread in Indian society. But it does not follow from this that denial of advancement to women or to Dalits is always due to social prejudice and never due to poor performance. In a central government office, in a public hospital or in an engineering college it is now often difficult to deny advancement to individuals from the weaker sections of society even when their performance is consistently below the average. Legitimate discrimination on the basis of ability and performance is obstructed by the pervasive suspicion that all discrimination, at least in India, is at bottom and by its nature invidious. Such an attitude tends to put ability and performance at a discount, and to act in the long run as an impediment to economic and social progress.

38

From Hierarchy to Equality

Jawaharlal Nehru had said on the eve of independence, 'The spirit of the age is in favour of equality, though practice denies it almost everywhere.' He then went on to declare, 'Yet the spirit of the age will triumph.' A good way to assess the changes that have taken place in the fifty years since independence will be to ask how far the country has progressed on the road to equality.

Almost immediately after independence, a number of important measures were adopted for securing greater equality among the people of the country. Principal among these were democracy based on adult suffrage, sweeping agrarian reform, and positive discrimination in favour of the Backward Classes. All of these have led to some gains for equality, but each of them has had many unexpected and unsuspected consequences. The important point is that the country has throughout this period never turned its back on the goal of greater equality. But the road to equality has revealed many snares and pitfalls that Nehru and his generation had not foreseen. Before independence, they had thought that all their projects were being callously thwarted by a hostile colonial regime, and that once they became masters of their own destiny, those projects would be realized at little cost. They had underestimated the capacity of an ancient hierarchical society to resist well-meaning attempts at radical change.

The hierarchical society inherited from the past may be likened to a gigantic iceberg of which only a small upper portion is visible above the waters, with its massive body resting below, frozen, immobile and submerged. In the warm environment created by independence, the ice has begun to melt, releasing swirls and eddies of incalculable force and momentum. Is it surprising that the gains of orderly progress appear again and again to be swept aside by massive outbursts of turbulence? It is a great mistake to believe that a hierarchical society can reconstitute itself on the basis of equality within a generation or two in a smooth and painless manner, without conflict, without violence.

It was natural for those who took over the governance of the country on independence to assume that politics and state power could be used for achieving their main social objectives. They greatly overestimated the transformative capacity of politics. It can certainly solve some problems, but not every kind of social problem. The indiscriminate use of politics for addressing every problem in society has now become a habit of mind with us. It delays and even obstructs processes of change that have their sources outside of politics and operate unnoticed across long stretches of time.

I do not wish to deny to politics its role in social transformation in general and in reducing social inequality in particular. We may, for example, consider land reform as a measure for reducing the inequalities between classes in which politics had a significant role. Agrarian reform had been a major political objective of the Congress party since before independence, and the legislation enacted in its furtherance after independence was voluminous. Many of those who had hoped for the complete elimination of unequal relations in agriculture were disappointed by the immediate effect of the reform. It is however clear in retrospect that the old feudal relations have steadily lost ground in the last fifty years. It is another matter that many of the expected gains of land reform were eaten up by massive increases in population throughout the 1950s, 1960s and 1970s.

Inequalities between individuals based on the distribution of land and other material resources is not the only problem faced on the road to equality. There are also massive disparities between castes that have existed since time immemorial. These too were matters of major concern for the leaders of the newly independent country. But attempts by successive governments to reduce caste disparities by political means have been less successful than agrarian reform. What the government did in fact was to take over the programme of quotas devised by the British, and then steadily expand the quotas in every direction. Many persons now realize that the gains to equality from the programme of reservations are small while the programme itself undermines the spirit of liberal democracy. But the quota mentality has in the meantime become firmly established, and no political party, whether of the left or the right, has the nerve to question it. Naturally, it will become further entrenched with the adoption of quotas for women.

To the extent that India's leaders were sincere in their commitment to equality at the time of independence, their mistake was to put so much emphasis on politics and so little on education. The gains from political intervention are often immediate and dramatic, but they as often evaporate without leaving much trace. The gains from education take time, a couple of generations at least, to become visible, but then they become permanently established.

The passage from hierarchy to equality can be made effective only by creating the widest range of open and secular institutions to which recruitment is based on individual ability and not birth in a particular caste or community. This comes with the emergence of a new occupational structure and a new educational system essential for its support. It is only through the joint operation of these two systems that the principle of equality of opportunity—or of careers open to talent—can be made socially effective.

In a society such as ours with its massive burden of inequalities inherited from the past, equality of opportunity cannot be effectively secured in a decade, or even a generation. For, real as against purely formal equality of opportunity depends not merely on the removal of disabilities but also on the creation of abilities. It is here that the role of education is decisive. In creating the kinds of abilities that are essential for a progressive economy and society, there is no substitute for a sound educational system. Instead of investing in education for all, we have tried to reduce disparities between castes through the short-cut of reservations. Our programme of reservations is perhaps the largest in the world, and our performance in primary and secondary education among the weakest. The gains to equality from reservation have been small, and, what is worse, we have failed to develop the human capital which alone can give substance to the principle of equality of opportunity in the long run.

It is not my argument that affirmative action should have no place at all in the overall plan for greater equality. But to be effective, it has to be administered sparingly and with restraint. Such programmes have indeed achieved good results in other countries, precisely because they have been used judiciously. In our case, particularly in the last twenty years, the programme has been buffeted around by political pressures to the point where it has become a threat to the very principle of equality of opportunity. The urge to find instant political solutions to deep-rooted and long-standing social problems may not be uniquely Indian. What does seem to be distinctively Indian is the faith in quotas, shared by conservatives and radicals alike, in solving all the problems of distribution and allocation.

39

The Checkerboard of Quotas

After the adoption of substantial quotas in public employment for backward castes and communities, there is the proposal now to have even more substantial quotas for women in parliament and in the state assemblies. There are also counter-proposals to have quotas within those quotas in favour of women belonging to the backward castes and the minority communities.

So far there are quotas only for the Scheduled Castes and the Scheduled Tribes in the services of the government as well as in the legislatures. The Other Backward Classes have quotas in the services but not in the legislatures; and the Women's Reservation Bill seeks quotas for women in the legislatures but not in the services. But as the momentum for justice through quotas gathers strength, demands for further reservations are bound to come up from those who have already secured some reservations. Indeed, if the demand to have quotas within the quotas for women is conceded, some seats in the Lok Sabha and the Vidhan Sabhas will be automatically earmarked for backward castes and communities.

If some of the seats earmarked for women in the legislatures come to be reserved on the basis of caste and community, it may be difficult in the long run to resist the demand that similar reservations be made for men as well. Again, if jobs in the government are reserved for the Other Backward Classes on the ground that they are disesteemed or unempowered, it will be difficult to oppose similar demands from women, once it has been conceded that, as a class, they too are without status and without power.

Our society is divided into innumerable groups, classes and categories. These divisions cut across each other, so that each division has its own subdivisions. Now that the demand for quotas has taken a hold on the public imagination, we can expect more and more groups, classes and categories to discover that they too are unempowered, disesteemed or disadvantaged in one respect or another, and hence entitled to their own quotas. The American political scientist Myron Weiner had once said to me light-heartedly that he was going to stand up one day and ask for a quota for left-handed Lithuanian Jews, for he could show that being left-handed, being a Jew and being of Lithuanian descent had been detrimental to his pursuit of life, liberty and happiness.

If the present trend continues, the public domain will be converted into a checkerboard of communities, classes and categories, each claiming its own specific entitlements. It is not clear how far our present constitution will be able to bear the weight of all these claims, for it is based on a concept of citizenship and of individual rights that is markedly at odds with the idea of entitlements promoted by the advocates of quota justice. One can hardly exaggerate the battering that the constitution will take if the demand for quotas and for quotas within quotas continues unchecked. It is well to remember that the first amendment to it had to be made barely a year after its adoption when the Madras High Court struck down caste quotas in medical education in Champakam Dorairajan's case.

The Women's Reservation Bill has brought to the surface the contradictions inherent in the theory of social justice through quotas. The demand for quotas on the basis of gender has come into direct collision with the entrenched claims for quotas on the basis of caste and community. It is an ineluctable social fact that the divisions of caste and community cut across those of gender. Every caste and community, from the lowest to the highest, has women as well as men; and women are no less heterogeneous than men in their affiliation to caste and community.

The argument that the distinctions of caste and class count only among men but not among women cannot be taken seriously by any student of Indian society. It may be a patriarchal myth that women are more status conscious than men; but it will be very hard to prove that they are less so. There was a spirit of generosity in the Constituent Assembly that had led to a general approval of quotas for the Scheduled Castes and Scheduled Tribes, groups that had been stigmatized and marginalized for centuries, if not millennia. That spirit of generosity has long since evaporated, and now it is each group for itself and the devil take the hindmost.

When there are quotas only on the basis of caste and community, women benefit far less than men because of the gender gap which is particularly wide among the Backward Classes. If there are quotas on the basis of gender only, they will be cornered by upper-caste women who are better educated, more experienced in public affairs and smarter by far than their lower-caste and Muslim counterparts. Certainly, the women who are arguing for themselves without distinction of caste and class come out much better on radio and television than their adversaries who are generally men belonging to the lower and intermediate castes and the Muslim community. But if the men often appear tedious and inarticulate, it has to be conceded that the women sometimes seem a little too smug.

We cannot evade the paradox of quotas. The advantages of group-based quotas go always to the least- and never to the most-disadvantaged individual members of the groups concerned. It is at this point that the iron enters the soul, for persons who are themselves well-off individually become the immediate beneficiaries of provisions created in the name of the dispossessed and the disinherited.

The disruption of the Lok Sabha over the Women's Reservation Bill in mid-July shocked many persons throughout the country. Yet it was naïve in the extreme for women parliamentarians to believe that they would be allowed to walk away with such a large prize without disturbance and without commotion. It is not simply that the consensus over the bill was a phoney consensus. More important than that, many of the leaders of the backward castes and the Muslims have deep-rooted fears that the political prizes that they have won for themselves, by fair means and foul, may be snatched away from them by underhand means in the name of women's empowerment.

Women have come to realize that men in politics can be very duplicitous, and now they openly say so. But they become very indignant when they find that in the eyes of the lower castes and the minorities, all upper-caste politicians, women as well as men, appear equally duplicitous. Where there is so much bad faith, one can hardly expect the other side to be taken in by expressions of injured innocence.

As things stand, the divisions are very sharp between those who want quotas for women only and those who want them especially for Backward Class and Muslim women. Each side has arguments against its opponents that appear to it to be unanswerable. Is there a solution to the problem? Compromises will no doubt be found, but they will be made in bad faith, and they will be unstable. The present crisis will have served some useful purpose only if it opens people's eyes a little to the threat posed to a rational and a secular constitution by the obsession with quotas.

40

The Meritarian Principle

Some time last winter the Harvard sociologist Nathan Glazer drew my attention to a public statement against the meritarian principle which had appeared in one of our national dailies. Glazer was intrigued by a misprint and asked if I knew what the word 'meritorian' meant. He was also intrigued by the names of the signatories, all intellectuals of great renown, including a couple known to both of us personally.

The meritarian principle is the one according to which benefits are distributed unequally among individuals according to merit, and not equally to all irrespective of ability or performance. It is a feature of societies marked by competition, innovation and change as against those marked by stability and adherence to traditional ways of life and socio-economic arrangements. The meritarian principle is at odds with caste and all socio-economic arrangements based on feudal, semi-feudal and quasi-feudal ties of patronage and dependence.

The meritarian principle is familiar to all college and university teachers, although it may not be equally cherished by all. It is difficult to see how a college or a university can function if students are not assessed and graded according to merit. I have known academics who scoff at the idea of merit

The Telegraph, 2 August 2002.

but use the strictest standards in admitting, promoting and awarding degrees to students; but there are also others who take these matters lightly. Where teachers take such matters lightly, students are inclined to believe that once they have secured admission they should all be awarded degrees, and some even feel that they should all be awarded first-class degrees. The meritarian principle has at best a limited appeal in a society in which patronage and dependence are so extensive.

It cannot be too strongly emphasized that the meritarian principle, or at least its salience, is a historical and not a universal phenomenon. It is salient in some societies and disregarded in others. Hence it may be unwise to make an assessment of it without regard for its social and historical context. There may be a case for restraining it in some social and historical contexts while encouraging it in others.

The meritarian principle as one expects it to operate in education and employment in our public institutions is, in a historical perspective, a modern phenomenon, going back barely two hundred years in time. It is modern, not just in the Indian context, but in the world as a whole. The principle was given a great impetus by the reforms introduced into France by Napoleon. Central to these reforms was the creation of the twin institutions of the great schools or the *grandes écoles* and the great services or the *grands corps*, recruitment to both of which was through open national competition.

Napoleon's ideas spread rapidly to other European countries, and then to other parts of the world. They acquired distinctive institutional forms as they spread from one part of the world to another. Our own University Grants Commission and Union Public Service Commission may be said to embody, each in its own way, the meritarian principle and the ideal of careers open to talent. Whether the problems these institutions now face arise from too much attention to the meritarian principle or a wilful disregard of that principle is a question that cannot be easily set aside.

Egalitarians in the nineteenth century and even later welcomed the meritarian principle which they believed to stand for equality of opportunity without consideration of birth, social origin or patronage. But doubts began to gradually arise about the social consequences of a single-minded application of the idea of careers open to talent. Talent or merit may be wrongly defined or wrongly assessed, and in that case the rewards of success or the penalties of failure might both turn out to be arbitrary and capricious. At the beginning of the twenty-first century, egalitarians have many more misgivings about the meritarian principle than they had at the beginning of the nineteenth or even the twentieth century.

A book published in 1958 by Michael Young with the title of *The Rise of Meritocracy* became a turning point in attitudes towards the meritarian principle among progressive intellectuals. Young drew pointed attention to the negative consequences of selection by merit as tested by competitive examinations. Many have come to believe that a single-minded attachment to the idea of merit as described above discourages diversity and stultifies creativity. It also fosters an unfeeling attitude towards those who fail in the competition, often through no fault of theirs, and are condemned as being without merit. There are social theorists who have warned against a 'callous meritocratic society'.

A meritocracy may be viewed as a system which carries the meritarian principle to its extreme limit by excluding all other social principles, such as amity, compassion, fellow-feeling, moderation and tolerance. But one does not need to be an advocate of meritocracy in order to appreciate and support the meritarian principle. The most common way of throwing cold water on it is to say that there is no agreed definition of merit and that it means different things to different persons. That is true but it hardly settles the matter. Most things that are of value are difficult to define, but that does not mean that we should not take them into account in the operation of institutions. Critics of the meritarian principle often say that what should count in the distribution of benefits and burdens is not merit but need. Need is indeed a consideration of the first importance; but then it is no more easy to define need than it is to define merit, for different persons have different conceptions not only of merit but also of need.

One does not need to have a general, formal and abstract definition of merit in order to grade MA examination papers or to select candidates for the civil service, without fear or favour, and in accordance with criteria agreed upon in advance. If merit is given short shrift in such cases, as it often is in India, it is not in order to meet some higher social objective but for the pettiest and the most mundane of reasons. The advocacy of the meritarian principle as well as its subversion are both tied to strategies of social mobility adopted by the same middle class. Those who aspire for mobility through individual initiative are inclined to favour the meritarian principle while those who expect to achieve it through collective political action tend to make light of it.

In India, white-collar trade unionism has acted as a strong force against the meritarian principle. My own first-hand experience of it is confined largely to the union of college and university teachers. The leaders of these unions have consistently taken the view that everybody should be promoted after the passage of a certain period of time and that nobody should be promoted—or even appointed—out of turn, meaning before the passage of the right amount of time. To the argument that merit, and not just seniority, should count, their response is that merit cannot be defined and that judgements of merit are by their nature arbitrary and capricious. They will take great comfort from the fact that there are some very eminent intellectuals who are on their side in debunking the principle of merit.

41

Public Institutions

Although it is widely if not universally endorsed and admired, democracy as a political system is still on trial in many parts of he world. This is true not only of the ex-colonial countries of Asia and Africa, but also of the transitional societies that emerged from the disintegration of the Soviet system in eastern and central Europe.

Today many people say that the success of democracy as a political system depends on the strength and vitality of the civil society on which it rests. However, the idea of civil society is both ambiguous and elastic. Political leaders, social activists, public intellectuals and even heads of international agencies call for the strengthening of civil society in the interest of democracy and development, but they have different agendas and different ideas about what they would like to strengthen.

Some put their stress on social movements which, they believe, will give direction to both democracy and development through increasingly wider participation in voluntary action and voluntary associations. Others point to the importance of stable and durable public institutions as essential requirements for the operation of a democratic society based on the rule of law. The ideas of civil society as social movement and as

The Telegraph, 6 January 2005.

public institutions are not contradictory, but their emphases are different.

Both Jawaharlal Nehru, independent India's first prime minister, and B.R. Ambedkar, the principal architect of the Constitution of India, were strong advocates of public institutions as the foundation of a democratic social order. The institutions that contribute most to the creation and strengthening of civil society are open and secular institutions. A large number of such institutions of a public or semi-public nature began to emerge in India from the middle of the nineteenth century onwards, and the viability of civil society has much to do with the health and well-being of those institutions.

Among the many institutions that contribute to the effective operation of civil society, I would like to pick out the university. The modern university is important in its own right and as an example of a new type of social arrangement based on a distinct set of ideas and values. The point I wish to make was nicely put by Nehru in his convocation address at the University of Allahabad delivered just after India's independence. He said, 'If the universities discharge their duty adequately, then it is well with the nation and the people,' and warned against the temple of learning being made 'a home of narrow bigotry and petty objectives'. Nehru was speaking of the university not just as a centre of knowledge and learning but also as the setting for a new kind of social existence.

A distinctive feature of the modern university as an institution is its socially inclusive nature. There were many institutions of learning in the past, but until the nineteenth century, they excluded individuals on the basis of race, caste, creed and gender. Although universities had existed in Europe continuously since the twelfth century, they began to become socially inclusive only in the second half of the nineteenth.

The Universities of Oxford and Cambridge, which were founded in the twelfth and thirteenth centuries, admitted only men and only Christians, and that too of the established church alone, until late in the nineteenth century. Our universities, which were founded in the second half of the nineteenth century, were socially inclusive from almost the very beginning. Sir Henry Maine, one of the early vice-chancellors of the University of Calcutta, observed in a convocation address in 1866, 'The fact is, that the founders of the University of Calcutta thought to create an *aristocratic* institution; and in spite of themselves, they created a *popular* institution.' Whereas it took Oxford and Cambridge six or seven hundred years to admit women to their degrees, the University of Calcutta was awarding degrees to women within a few decades of its foundation. By the end of the nineteenth century, the days of the university as an 'aristocratic' or socially exclusive institution were coming to an end. Many modern institutions of different kinds have followed broadly the same course, though with varying degrees of success, in India and elsewhere throughout the twentieth century.

I would like to stress that the idea of the university as an open and secular institution, or a socially inclusive one, is a modern rather than a Western idea. For the better part of their historical existence, Western universities were highly exclusive. It was only with the coming of modern times that first Western, and then most universities began to be inclusive in their social outlook.

While the modern university must be socially inclusive, it has to be academically discriminating. The proper discharge of its academic as well as social responsibilities requires it to discriminate among both students and teachers, fairly and impartially, according to ability and performance. Such discrimination is vital to the proper functioning not only of the university but of any modern institution, whether a public hospital or public corporation. Social movements that seek to do away with all considerations of ability and performance in public institutions do not enhance but diminish the vitality of civil society.

It is easy enough to distinguish in principle between discrimination on social grounds, that is, on the basis of race, caste, gender, and so on, and discrimination on functional grounds, that is, on the basis of ability and performance. But it is often difficult to do so in practice, and sometimes the consequences of the second or desirable kind of discrimination appear to be much the same as those of the first or undesirable kind. Again, this may be illustrated by taking the example of the modern university.

In India, the modern university has to operate in a social environment that is permeated by vast disparities between regions, among castes and communities, and between men and women. If we apply the same high academic standards rigidly and inflexibly, large sections of the population will remain excluded, or virtually excluded, from the benefits of higher education. There is no reason why all universities in a large and very diverse country should have exactly the same academic standards for evaluating the performance of either their students or their teachers. A good university should look a little like the society in which it exists; hence, if academic standards have to be relaxed to some extent in the interest of social diversity, that in itself should not jeopardize its contribution to civil society. The same would hold true by and large for any public institution.

However, the claim of diversity, or any other claim made on behalf of the larger society, cannot set at naught the specific requirements of the university as an academic institution. Academic standards may be relaxed in the larger social interest up to a point, but they cannot be stretched indefinitely or arbitrarily without depriving the university of its focus and undermining its legitimacy. Public institutions have particular functions to perform, and they must perform those functions well, or at least adequately, if they are to contribute to the well-being of civil society. Democracy as a political system cannot work properly if the institutions of civil society are in continuous disarray and lose all their credibility.

42

Quotas for Companies

By creating expectations about reservations in the private sector, the Congress party has raised the stakes in competitive populism to new heights. The left parties have not lagged behind in demanding their pound of flesh from the capitalist class. Whatever the similarities may be in the social and political consequences of reservations in the public and private sectors, their legal and constitutional implications are bound to be very different.

Reservations in the private sector will mark a new departure in the making of public policy. All policy making requires the balancing of conflicting aims and interests, and the policy of reservations is no exception. The policy of caste quotas in employment was devised by the colonial administration, and first applied in peninsular India in the early 1920s. The colonial policy was driven by two different objectives: the political objective of creating a new balance of power and the humanitarian objective of promoting equality and social justice. The nationalist leadership, which at that time took a negative view of caste and communal quotas, was not prepared to credit the colonial administration with any humanitarian objective, and saw the quotas as part of a policy of divide and rule.

The Telegraph, 12 October 2004.

Opponents of caste quotas in the colonial period had hoped that they would be scaled down after independence. Instead, they have been scaled up. It cannot be that the British advocated caste quotas only on political grounds and the leaders of independent India advocate it only on humanitarian grounds. Many now feel that political considerations have been uppermost in the extension of caste quotas since the time of the Mandal Commission of 1979–80. But the movement for reservations would not have had such continuing success if it did not strike a chord in the hearts and minds of those who yearn for greater equality and social justice.

Simply because it is widely believed that caste quotas reduce inequality, it does not follow that they in fact do so. Inequality has many different faces. It is not easy to determine whether inequality overall has increased or decreased in the last fifty years, leave alone the contributions made by different factors to its increase or decrease. But to say that the social effects of the policy of reservations are difficult to measure is not to imply that it has had no social effect.

Perhaps the most durable effect of the policy is its contribution to a change in the social composition of the Indian middle class. The colonial administrators who introduced the policy did not see beyond the middle class; they were certainly not trying to create a policy for the revolutionary transformation of Indian society. It is not a very convincing argument that scaling up caste-based reservations further by extending them to private employment will lead to a radical transformation of the social structure.

Despite its undeniable social and political significance, the middle class comprised a relatively small section of the Indian population at the time of independence. It has become much larger and much more differentiated in the last fifty years. It is now important not only socially and politically, but also demographically. The middle class grew first with the expansion of the public sector and then with the opening of the market. A large and vibrant middle class, equipped with professional, administrative, managerial, technical and even clerical skills and abilities is an asset to any society and indispensable to a constitutional democracy. And the more diverse the middle class is in its social composition, the more effectively it is likely to play its political role.

It has to be emphasized that the expansion and diversification of the middle class has come about through the operation of a number of different factors. State actions in general and preferential policies in particular have undoubtedly made their contribution. In both absolute and relative terms there are many more members of the Scheduled Castes, the Scheduled Tribes and the Other Backward Classes in the Indian middle class than there were fifty years ago. At the same time this diversification would not have taken place without far-reaching changes in the economy, and it cannot be sustained if it is pursued as an inflexible policy without attention to the demands of the economy.

It may be a good thing for private firms to have managers, technicians, office assistants and others from a wider rather than a narrower range of castes and communities. Some companies may wish to change their strategies of recruitment in that direction in their own long-term interest. But it is difficult to see how in a political system that protects private property and the freedom of enterprise the state can dictate to a private company the nature of the social composition of its employees. It can at best encourage companies to adopt socially sensitive strategies of recruitment by offering them tax concessions and other incentives. And companies can make their own contribution by creating facilities for the education and training of talented individuals from socially disadvantaged communities.

In reviewing the legal and constitutional aspects of preferential policies, it is essential to keep in mind the distinction between mandatory and enabling provisions. Mandatory provisions, like the one relating to the reservation of seats in the Lok Sabha under Article 330 of the constitution, are those that must be applied. Enabling provisions, like the one under Article 16(4) relating to reservations in employment, are those that may be applied, depending upon conditions and circumstances. Enabling provisions are necessary where preferential policies may be challenged on the ground that they appear inconsistent with other provisions, such as those relating to equality of opportunity.

The Indian policy of reservations has often been compared with the American policy of affirmative action, but the differences are deeper than the similarities. In the United States, even when the environment was most favourable to affirmative action, the provisions for it were enabling and not mandatory. The state did not order or instruct the University of California or the University of Michigan to have preferential policies. The universities made their own provisions and then pleaded with the courts to allow the provisions to stand, arguing that they did not violate any basic principle of law. The Indian situation is quite different. Reservations in education and employment operate through orders of the government prescribing numerical quotas which the US courts would never uphold.

In India, supporters of preferential policies have acquired the habit of thinking only in terms of numerical quotas and mandatory provisions. But the government cannot impose on firms and companies its own preferences regarding the social composition of employees on private contract without violating basic legal and economic principles. On the one hand, the government wants to free the economy from the control of the state so that it can work according to economic and not bureaucratic principles. On the other, its initiatives on reservations in the private sector will lead to the control of hiring and firing to an extent not contemplated even in the heyday of the command economy. Hiring and firing can be either regulated by the market or controlled by the state. It is difficult to see how both things can be done at the same time.

43

Affirmative Action Revisited

My attention was drawn by the two-part article on affirmative action published in these columns on 1 and 2 May by the distinguished American sociologist Nathan Glazer. The American programme of affirmative action is once again in the public eye on account of the Michigan case discussed by Glazer in the article referred to, and more extensively in an article in *The New York Review of Books* of 15 May by the well-known jurist and proponent of affirmative action, Ronald Dworkin. The Indian programme, never too far from the public eye since the Mandal agitations of 1990, has been given a new twist by the emerging political consensus to extend reservations to the 'weaker sections' among the 'forward castes'.

Parallels have been drawn between the American programme of racial preferences and the Indian programme of caste quotas, although this has been done mainly by Indians and rarely by Americans. Over the years, I have been struck more by the differences than by the similarities between the American and the Indian experiences. At the same time, we learn as much about ourselves from others when they are different as we learn from them when they are similar.

In reading the articles by Glazer and by Dworkin, I was

---

struck by the similarity not only of argument but also of tone even though Dworkin has been a consistent supporter of racial preferences whereas Glazer has been at best a sceptic. They write calmly and analytically, leaving it largely to the reader to form his own judgement. Indians, on the other hand, tend to write passionately if not stridently; but whether it is academic prose or judicial prose, the passion is often only a thin cover for the weakness of the argument.

The Indian programme of caste quotas has a much longer history than the American programme of racial preferences, and it has much wider constitutional, legal and political implications. Political calculations entered into it from the beginning, but in the past there were other considerations as well. Since 1990 it has been driven almost entirely by political considerations. Political parties, blocs and factions support it vociferously in public but run it down in private whenever their interest requires them to do so. Nothing has brought this out more clearly than the sordid saga of the Women's Reservation Bill.

In the United States even when racial preferences were being used most extensively and openly, there were misgivings about fixing quotas proportionate to population. What the American experience has taught me is the importance of the distinction between affirmative action, which I consider to be desirable not only in America but also in India, and numerical quotas which I consider to be pernicious. But there is no getting away from numerical quotas so long as the agenda in such matters is set by politicians and their administrative underlings.

The agenda for affirmative action in university admissions was set in the US by the university and not the state. Glazer stresses the active part played by the universities themselves in creating their own affirmative action programmes. 'These policies for the most part were adopted voluntarily by each institution. Neither the Federal nor the State Government requires this preference for blacks.' If there was pressure for adopting racial preferences, it came from militant black students. The universities tried out affirmative action in a small way in the 1960s and 1970s, and found that it worked. Presidents and deans of such reputed universities as Harvard and Princeton took up the case for affirmative action. Glazer believes that even if the US Supreme Court rules against the specific policy adopted by the University of Michigan, American universities will find some way of continuing with affirmative action without violating the letter of the law.

In India, academic institutions do not value or even understand their autonomy sufficiently to take the initiative in such matters. They wait for directives from the government and then decide whether to implement them or take evasive action. Again, the Women's Reservation Bill brings out this point very nicely. The left parties have been chafing at the bit over the inadequate representation of women in the legislatures. But why do they have to wait for a constitutional amendment to make their representation more adequate? What has prevented them from fielding more women candidates for election to the legislatures or from selecting talented women for key posts in the party? The leadership of no party really believes that there is any need for more women in the legislatures, but it will not say so openly for fear of losing their votes in the next election.

In the United States, the case for racial preferences in student admissions is made from the argument for diversity rather than equality. Those responsible for the governance of the top universities have come to feel that it is not good for their universities to be wholly monochromatic, that it is better for them to look a little more like America. As each university has sought to gradually enhance its diversity in its own way and at its own pace, support for such programmes has spread through the university system. Presidents and deans support affirmative action because they believe that it will do good to their universities in the long run and not because they expect it to rectify all the injuries inflicted on disadvantaged groups in the past.

Both supporters and opponents of affirmative action in America recognize that it entails some cost to the principle of selection by individual merit alone. The supporters are prepared to pay the price, which they do not consider to be too high, in the interest of diversity which they consider to be good for their institution. The opponents are not prepared to pay the price because they believe that it serves no useful purpose to have more blacks or more Hispanics than can come in through open competition. Here, I am on the side of the supporters because I believe that diversity in a public institution is desirable even at some cost to selection by merit, but not at any cost.

In the US, support for racial preference is based on arguments about policy and not about rights. In India the distinction between matters of policy and matters of right has been steadily and, if I may add, wilfully obscured, and the language of rights is used in season and out of season in order to keep the political temperature up.

Ronald Dworkin, who is perhaps the most outstanding intellectual proponent of affirmative action, has always made his case on grounds of policy and never on grounds of right. Commenting on the policy of racial preferences adopted by the medical school of the University of California at Davis, he had argued that there was no violation of individual rights, and that the question of rights did not arise. Allen Bakke did not have a right of admission simply because his test scores were adequate. He did have the right to be considered, and the right not to be rejected on arbitrary and capricious grounds. His application was in fact given due consideration but it had to be rejected in the interest of a good policy, so the ground for his rejection could not be attacked as arbitrary or capricious.

The constitutional, legal and political climate in the United States is different from what it is in India. Americans are extremely reluctant to amend their constitution; Indian politicians think nothing of amending theirs so long as they have the numbers on their side. C. Rajagopalachari, perhaps the most far-seeing among the leaders of the nationalist movement, drew repeated attention to this contrast, and never tired of warning his countrymen of the disastrous consequences of allowing the constitution to become a plaything of politicians. Rajaji had the clarity, the conviction and the courage to speak his mind, even when he came to realize that his was probably a cry in the wilderness. Even to mention his name in this context is to realize how low our political leadership has sunk in its moral and intellectual calibre.

VII
State and Civil Society

It is obvious that, despite its many travails, democracy has come to stay in India. Democracy is of course a set of political institutions but there are social preconditions for the successful functioning of those institutions. The challenge in India is to build a working democracy in a society which is permeated by hierarchical values and institutions.

After independence the newly created republican state was expected to play a leading part in transforming a poor, backward and stagnant society into a prosperous and vibrant one. There is now widespread disillusion with the state and the misuse of power by its functionaries; but the state continues to be an important institution that cannot be kept out of the reckoning in any serious discussion of democracy and development.

It has become common to contrast the negative features of the state with the positive ones of civil society. But the public discussion of civil society lacks a proper focus, and the term has come to mean all things to all persons. Some put voluntary action and voluntary associations at the core of civil society, and there has indeed been a great proliferation of NGOs in recent years in India and many other countries of the world. It is difficult to determine how lasting the contributions of these organizations will be. In the view adopted here the core of civil society consists of the open and secular institutions that link citizens to the state and to each other.

44

Democracy and Development

Is democracy good for development? Few would dare to answer in the negative, and many would hesitate even to raise the question. Most persons believe that democracy is a good thing and so is development, and that therefore the two must move hand in hand. Yet the relationship between democracy and development is an extremely complex one, as we can easily see from a comparison of the experiences of the different countries in our own continent.

India and China have been compared and contrasted repeatedly over the last fifty years. India's record of democracy has been exceptional in the non-Western world. There have been regular elections at every level from the village panchayat to the national parliament, involving a plurality of parties. The rule of law has been sustained by a sound constitution and a responsible judiciary. It is true that the elections have not always been free or fair, and that the law is violated regularly and persistently, but few would seriously question the significance and value of these institutions. There has been on the whole little official restraint on the free flow of information or on open public debate and discussion.

China's record of democracy has, by contrast with India's,

The Telegraph, 11 December 1998.

been exceedingly poor. Not only was there no plurality of parties and, hence, no elections in any meaningful sense, but the rule of law was and to this day remains very weakly developed. If democracy means the tolerance of dissent, that was effectively suppressed during the long reign of Chairman Mao, and dissenting voices are barely audible even now. No two countries could be more unlike than China and India so far as the public expression of dissent is concerned.

The suppression of the free flow of information and of public dissent has been responsible for untold human suffering in China. The most dramatic example of this suffering, now widely acknowledged both within and outside the country, was that caused by the famines which took millions of lives. It is unlikely that famines on such a scale could cause so much loss of life in an open and democratic society, no matter how meagre its material resources. The press and public opinion would see to it that the government moved food supplies to the worst-affected areas. The people would be far less passive and the authorities far less callous in India than in China. Where free institutions exist, no government can expect to survive if it turns its back upon massive human suffering, and this undoubtedly is a good thing for development, no matter how we define the term.

Although India may take pride in its performance as a free and open society, its record of development in the last fifty years leaves much to be desired. At least in Asia, and particularly in East Asia, many far less democratic countries have done rather better. And this will stand true even if we set aside such crude indicators of development as per capita income and look instead at more basic indicators such as safe drinking water, primary health care and elementary education. The institutions that give protection from famine do not necessarily ensure the rapid spread of either elementary education or primary health care. Perhaps we will learn something about how democracy works in the real world if we ask why a country that has fared reasonably well in combating famine has fared so badly in endowing its ordinary citizens with certain basic capabilities.

It would be pleasing to believe that the basic amenities of life are always more easily secured under democratic than under authoritarian regimes. This obviously is not the case in every phase of development. China provides only the extreme example: Korea, Malaysia and even Indonesia have done rather better in regard to basic health and education under more or less authoritarian regimes than has India with its manifestly superior record of democratic freedoms.

However much we may deplore the lack of democratic freedoms in authoritarian regimes, we should not believe that they have no interest whatever in the health and well-being of their people. They have their own interest, including the desire for industrial and military power, in their people even when they lack a strong sense of accountability to them. Ordinary people do not always create their own capabilities, and others do not create capabilities in them from motives that are entirely laudable.

In a democracy, the creation of capabilities is a slow and uneven process, subject to many conflicting pulls and pressures. Authoritarian regimes are often effective levellers of social distinctions even though they maintain marked inequalities of power between the rulers and the ruled. The democratic process does not eliminate social distinctions; it only moderates and rearranges them.

Democratic regimes allow room not only for the expression of dissent but also for the organization and articulation of divergent social interests. Those who are better organized and more articulate always have an advantage in a democracy.

The middle class in particular is able to use its material, cultural and social capital to promote its own interests more effectively in democratic than in authoritarian regimes. An authoritarian regime can give short shrift to the demands of the middle class as and when it chooses. A democratic regime has to be more mindful of those demands even when they appear unreasonable and contrary to the general interest.

The growth of democratic institutions such as an elected parliament, an independent judiciary and a free press has been associated everywhere with the ascendancy of the middle class, and everywhere the middle class has been well served by democracy. Everywhere, and not just in India, it projects its own interest as the interest of society as a whole. The only difference is that in India the middle class comprises a smaller segment of the total population than it does in the advanced industrial societies, and hence it appears to be more self-serving here than elsewhere. Throughout the Western world, the middle class secured its own position first before ensuring the spread of the basic facilities of health and education in the population as a whole. In a democracy, it will be naïve to expect the middle class to promote the general interest before first securing its particular interest.

Elementary education, primary health care and other things essential for building up the capabilities of the most disadvantaged sections of society are not very high among the priorities of the middle class. It is not that the middle class is opposed to these things, but simply that it will not take to the streets if they are neglected as it will do if fees are raised for college and university students and salaries are not enhanced for teachers, doctors and others in public employment. It is true that in a democracy a government may fall if it does nothing while a famine is raging. But it may also fall if it deprives the urban middle class in order to attend to the rural poor. This does not mean that the benefits of democracy are only for the well-to-do and not for the disadvantaged; it only means that the latter have to wait longer for the benefits to reach them.

45

Civil Society and Voluntary Action

There has been growing talk in recent years about civil society and what it can contribute towards making individual and collective life more effective and more fruitful. In earlier decades, one did not hear much talk about civil society, except among Marxists and, even there, mainly those Marxists who drew their inspiration from Gramsci rather than Lenin. Today many more persons, of diverse political persuasions, talk about civil society, although that does not mean that they are all talking about the same thing.

Fifty years ago, enlightened Indians gave much more attention to the state and the public sector than to civil society. When intellectuals thought of society, they usually thought of it as something backward that needed to be changed through bold and responsible state action. There was a kind of consensus then that the state should take the lead in moving society forward by taking charge of the commanding heights of the economy.

Today the state has lost its shine to such an extent that it is difficult to imagine how much was expected of it by even the most balanced and judicious public intellectuals at the time of independence. Part of the reason for the disenchantment

The Telegraph, 5 November 1999.

lay in the very high expectations about the transformative powers of the state. Its actual performance was at best indifferent, and the Emergency and its aftermath showed it to be both oppressive and ineffectual. The poor performance of the state and people's low expectations of it began to reinforce each other.

The disenchantment spread from the state and its organs— the legislature, the bureaucracy and the judiciary—to other public institutions. Today all political parties are viewed with mistrust if not contempt, sometimes even by their own members. It is in this light that we have to view the appeal of civil society and the divergent ideas that have emerged about what it is and what it ought to be.

What is civil society? Clearly, it cannot be the same thing as state, or religion, or family. It may overlap with these to a certain extent, but it has, by common consent, a distinctive identity of its own. Beyond this, there is disagreement about the defining features of civil society. I assign central importance to a plurality of open and secular institutions, each enjoying a measure of autonomy. But a more common practice seems to be to treat voluntary action and voluntary associations—what in India are called non-governmental organizations or NGOs— as the defining features of civil society.

The value of individual initiative and voluntary action for the growth and success of democracy cannot be too strongly emphasized. Excessive reliance on the state in the early decades of independence dampened voluntary action and individual initiative. But the state only reinforced and did not create habits of mind already present in a caste- and kin-based hierarchical society.

Alexis de Tocqueville was the first important political theorist to dwell on the significance of voluntary action and voluntary associations for the democratic way of life. He was greatly struck by the voluntary associations he saw in the United States where they were more numerous, more diverse and more vigorous than anywhere in Europe. In his oft-quoted words, 'Wherever at the head of some new undertaking you see the government in France, or a man of rank in England, in the United States you will be sure to find an association.' He believed that the Americans had a special knack for creating and sustaining associations which the French lacked, and that was one reason why democracy was more successful in America than in France.

Do we in India have a special aptitude for creating and sustaining voluntary associations? Going by the enormous proliferation of NGOs in the last two decades, one might say that we do. But in such matters we cannot go by numbers alone. We must know a little more about how they are started, organized and supported, and the mechanisms by which they seek to ensure their continuity.

It is difficult to be categorical on these questions because NGOs differ greatly among themselves, and the material we have on them is fragmentary and ambiguous. The component of voluntary action is not equally strong in all NGOs: not all of them are supported fully or even mainly by resources raised by their own members from among themselves. Funding is often provided by external agencies that have at best only a sympathetic interest, but no direct involvement, in the work of the NGOs concerned. The donors include foreign agencies and even ministries of the union and state governments. I was told by a perceptive young sociologist in Chandigarh that there were very few NGOs in the Punjab since it had the unfortunate reputation of being a prosperous state.

When an NGO and a department of the government work in the same field, there is sometimes a healthy rivalry which, if kept under control, might act to the general advantage. An interesting development in India, which would perhaps have puzzled Tocqueville, is the tendency among senior functionaries of the state to start their own NGOs after retirement. They are able to attract funds and also to provide valuable financial, legal and administrative expertise. It is no wonder that some NGOs are very well run and show the kind of flexibility one cannot expect from a Byzantine government bureaucracy.

A well-run association providing useful services to the public does not become an institution unless it is able to ensure its continuity over time. The lifespan of an institution is expected to extend beyond the lives of its individual members. It is too early to say as yet how successfully the NGOs that have proliferated in recent years will outlive the persons by whom they were set up. The problem of succession is a very crucial one in institutions. The civil service has the advantage of continuously recruiting new members and promoting or retiring old ones through impersonal rules. Our political parties have been less successful in ensuring succession through impersonal rules, and tend to fall back on the family for replacing deceased leaders by new ones.

The natural tendency in India is for family and kinship to become implicated in the organization of voluntary action. In an increasing number of cases, the wife, the son or the daughter-in-law takes over the running of an NGO set up by a person of energy and vision. This is very different from the way in which open and secular institutions are expected to conduct their affairs. The civil service, for all its shortcomings, has at least managed to ensure recruitment, promotion and retirement without bringing family and kinship into the picture. The Congress party has provided an object lesson to the country by its complete failure to ensure institutional succession at the top without recourse to the genealogical principle. Which one of these models will the NGOs follow? An NGO that becomes a new kind of family business cannot contribute very much to the building of a healthy civil society.

46

The Third Sector

The non-governmental organization or NGO has emerged as an important feature of the Indian social landscape, and the last decade of the twentieth century may justly be described as the decade of the NGO. This development is not confined to India. It is a worldwide phenomenon, although it has become particularly conspicuous in the less developed countries of Asia, Africa and Latin America. In some of these countries, the NGO is seen as the main driving force in economic development and social change. NGOs are now active in practically every field; literacy, education, health, sanitation childcare, nutrition, habitation, and so on.

There is also a growing body of literature on NGOs, although much of this takes the form of advocacy rather than detached and objective analysis. Here they are coming to be represented as the Third Sector of society in which the state and the market are viewed as the first and the second sectors. This is a very large claim, for there are a great many things in the life of a society that are not covered by the state or the market, and it is doubtful that NGOs, no matter how numerous or versatile, can do all the things that are not done by the state or the market.

The NGO is distinct from the state because it is a 'non-

The Times of India, 10 March 2000.

governmental organization'; it is distinct from the market because it is a 'non-profit organization'. But there are many institutions in contemporary Indian society, such as the University of Delhi, the National Library or the Indian Institute of Science that cannot be justly described as creatures of either the state or the market. To the extent that it is inferred that the functions of such institutions can be better performed by NGOs, that inference is false and needs to be repudiated.

The advocacy of NGOs has grown in part from the disenchantment with the state and the statutory institutions that depend for support on it. Some have turned that disenchantment into enthusiasm for the market, and others into enthusiasm for the NGO. In the decades immediately following independence, the state, by overextending itself and its bureaucratic apparatus, stifled both economic and social initiative. In seeking to take over the commanding heights of the economy, it created a regime of licences, controls and permits which left less and less room for initiative in economic action. In seeking to extend its patronage to all sectors of society, it narrowed the space for voluntary effort in autonomous institutions.

No one will deny the great significance of voluntary action in the life of a democratic society. To the extent that they release the impulse for it, voluntary associations and non-governmental organizations make a valuable contribution to public life. But it will be a mistake to believe that there is room for individual initiative and voluntary effort in only the NGO and none in the university, the laboratory or the hospital. The universities in India, no matter how debased their present condition, are neither governmental organizations nor organizations for profit. If they and other public institutions of their kind have failed to live up to our expectations, that does not mean that they must now be written off, and public support and sympathy directed away from them and into the NGOs.

Voluntary action, if it is to be socially effective, must acquire some kind of organizational form. When an association becomes successful and expands its activities, it has to contend with the problems inherent in all organizations, namely, administration, funding and accounting. These present challenges to its self-reliance and autonomy. In the Nehru era, universities and other public institutions yielded all too easily to the temptations of official patronage, and expanded beyond their capacity to deal with the objectives they were created to achieve. They thundered about autonomy, but did everything that leads institutional autonomy to be undermined.

In the larger social perspective, institutional autonomy can only be relative, and never absolute. Every institution does not need to be autonomous in every respect, but it has to safeguard its autonomy in those respects that are crucial to its chosen or designated form of activity. Too much should not be made of the need for financial autonomy in public institutions. The universities of England and Holland have maintained substantial autonomy in teaching and research, despite having to depend on the state for funding. On the other hand, the NGOs themselves do not secure all their funds from the voluntary contributions for their own members. They depend for funds on the government, and, increasingly, on international agencies. Their autonomy from the agencies on which they depend for financial support cannot simply be taken on trust.

There are other questions besides those relating to the sources of funding. While it is true that the component of voluntary action in our public institutions has steadily declined, it is also true that that component is not equally strong in all voluntary associations. In some NGOs the component of voluntary action is very weak indeed. In a landmark study in Britain, Lord Beveridge had pointed out that voluntary action is propelled by two distinct motives, which he called the mutual aid motive and the philanthropic motive. There is not much evidence of the salience of the mutual aid motive in the working of NGOs in India. As to the philanthropic motive, that is more readily directed into religious than into secular institutions. Where NGOs in India have benefited from the philanthropic motive, the philanthropy has come more often from outside than from within India.

In the end, while the claim that the NGOs constitute the Third Sector of society has to be taken with a large pinch of salt, it still remains true that many of them are engaged in useful and productive work. There are many things that the government could have done for the people, but did not do or did badly. If the NGOs can do some of these things and do them better than the government, they deserve public support and sympathy. But if an excess of zeal for their actual or possible contributions leads to a continuous and wholesale denigration of the work done by the agencies of the government and by autonomous and semi-autonomous institutions, or to the withdrawal of public support and sympathy from them, that will act against the well-being of society.

47

Development as a Human Right

The prospects—and the failures—of development have haunted public-spirited Indians since the time of independence. At that time everyone or almost everyone believed that development was both a desirable and an attainable objective. Since then it has turned out to be a rather more elusive phenomenon. At first the insufficiency of material resources and the difficulty of mobilizing them appeared as the main constraints. Thereafter the very concept of development as it was initially used began to be challenged as vague, ill-defined and self-contradictory. Soul-searching about what development means or ought to mean has by no means come to an end.

The year 1977, which marked the end of the Emergency and the installation of the first non-Congress government in Delhi, was a watershed not only in India's political life but also in its intellectual life. A new government wanted a break with the past, and there were intellectuals who came forward with the promise of a new approach. The late 1970s and early 1980s brought to the fore the concept of alternatives: development alternatives and even alternatives of development. An element of national pride was involved in the slogan of alternatives to the extent that it set itself against the slavish

The Times of India, 26 January 2001.

imitation of Western models. In fact development economists had known all along that Indian problems had many unique features and not much would be achieved by blindly following either the American or the Russian path.

Long before the talk of development alternatives or alternatives to development gained currency, it was realized within the Planning Commission itself that development was not simply a matter of increasing the gross national product. Distribution was as important as growth, and the question was how to balance the requirements of the two when they were in conflict. Nobody either within or outside the Planning Commission had suggested that growth should be pursued at any cost, no matter how adversely it affected distribution. But it was also agreed that the size of the cake had to increase for a reasonable distribution of it to be possible. It would be disingenuous to pretend that the concern for equity or even equality appeared on the horizon only after 1977.

It is one thing to say that the demands of growth be harmonized with those of distribution or that the social costs of economic growth should be minimized, and quite another to design policies that will achieve those ends. Again, it is one thing to fashion attractive policies and quite another to ensure their implementation. Indians have never been at a loss to fashion attractive policies; it is the will to implement them that has been lacking.

The talk about alternatives discredited the idea of development for a while, but it could not destroy it. Development is bound to remain a major preoccupation in a country in which there is so much destitution, hunger, illiteracy and ill-health and such extremes of wealth and poverty. But there has been a change in the discourse on development. Whereas in the 1950s and 1960s development was discussed mainly in the language of policy, today it is being increasingly discussed in the language of rights.

Several factors have contributed to the shift from the language of policy to the language of rights in the current discussion of development. The persistent failures of policy have led to a loss of faith in the executive government, first in the political executive and soon after in the administrative executive. Policy is the main responsibility of the executive, and where there is a loss of faith in the executive there is bound to be a loss of faith in policy. This may be seen with regard to elementary education. The constitution decided it should be a matter of policy; now through an amendment to it, elementary education is being made into a right. Other rights will no doubt be created and the constitution suitably amended to give them recognition.

There has been a change in the climate of international opinion. The United Nations and other international agencies have become spokesmen for human rights, particularly in what used to be called the less developed countries. The NGOs, often with strong international support, are also inclined towards rights as against policies on the ground that whereas policies are the creatures of governments, rights empower the people.

The United Nations has recently taken the initiative to promote a rights-based approach to development. It has called for a worldwide recognition of the right to development and for that right to be treated as a human right. Some have welcomed this as a fresh approach to development. But it is not very clear as to what this might imply apart from a declaration of intent. Will the creation of new rights be accompanied by the creation and redistribution of material resources? Will the United Nations secure the resources to make the new rights effective?

In a constitutional democracy rights are a serious matter. They cannot be created simply in order to give expression to good intentions. The creation of rights that remain unenforced and are perhaps unenforceable damages the fabric of democracy. If we adopt the right to development as a human right, who will be the bearers of the right: individuals, classes, communities or nations? How will the right be enforced? Where there is a right there must be a court in which one can seek redress when the right to development has been violated. Perhaps all that one will be able to do in the event of default will be to appeal to the conscience of the world. But in that case will it have been worthwhile to have wilfully set at naught the very wise distinction made in the Indian constitution between matters of right and matters of policy?

If policies are the main responsibility of the executive, rights are the main responsibility of the judiciary. Our courts are already overburdened with litigation, including public interest litigation. The creation of new rights will increase the burden on the courts and it will encourage judges with an activist bent of mind to adopt an increasingly interventionist stance. Nothing can be more ominous for our fragile democracy than for the judiciary to seek to appropriate the functions of the executive on the ground that the latter is corrupt, inefficient and uncaring.

48

The Executive and the Judiciary

There has been growing concern over the failure of governance in the last couple of decades. It is felt that the country has vast resources, human as well as material, and that poor governance has caused them to be squandered or kept idle. Lack of development is now attributed more to the failure of governance than to the scarcity of resources. The concern over governance is not only felt within the less developed countries, it is increasingly expressed by international agencies, particularly those responsible for providing financial assistance to those countries.

When people point to the failures of governance, what they mainly have in mind is the executive government which is responsible for the formulation as well as the implementation of policy. Sometimes it is the policy itself that is found wanting, but more often it is the inadequate, half-hearted and one-sided implementation of it that is the target of attack. It is long since I have heard any public intellectual in India speak in praise of the executive government of the country.

I use the term 'executive' in the broad sense to include both the political and the administrative executive, that is, the ministry as well as the civil service. The division of tasks between the two is complex and cannot be fixed with any degree of

The Hindu, 8 May 2001.

precision. In principle, the secretary is subordinate to his minister, but this does not mean that he is dispensable or can be treated lightly. It is impossible to conduct a modern system of governance without files, and he who has mastery of the files has a powerful weapon in his hands. The minister can certainly overrule the advice of his secretary, but in a healthy democracy the reason for doing so has to be recorded in the file.

It is natural and healthy for intellectuals to keep the establishment under scrutiny and to expose its misdeeds. This after all is the essence of democracy, and it is in the long-term interest of the establishment itself. Open and regular criticism provides a safety valve against the accumulation of secret and subterranean resentment with its incalculable destructive potential for state and civil society. But criticism of any organ of society becomes counterproductive when it leads to a steady demoralization of its members. It cannot be said that the morale of our administrative executive is very high today; it has begun to show signs of loss of nerve that does not augur well for Indian democracy.

There is no doubt that the executive itself is largely responsible for the low esteem in which it is held by the public. Here the political executive has shown the way. There has been a steady decline in the ability and integrity of our ministers. It is true that not all ministers in Nehru's time were men of unshakeable integrity; but the lack of integrity—or ability—was not as openly on display as it is today. Many ministers, like the nabobs under the East India Company, amass great wealth and lead lives of conspicuous luxury. Not all ministers are profligate or irresponsible, but there are enough of those to put the political executive as a whole under a shadow.

Even the best of civil servants will find it hard to contend with the kinds of ministers we now have, and the best among our young men and women are turning away from the civil service. The administrative executive works in an adverse environment, and many of its members learn to adapt to that environment instead of resisting it in the public interest. The relationship between the political and the administrative executives, though close and intimate, is fraught with tension. The general belief in an unholy alliance between ministers and civil servants hardly adds to the latter's self-esteem.

Of the various organs of the state, it is the judiciary which has maintained its dignity in the public eye most effectively. Ordinary people look up to judges in a way in which they no longer look up to legislators, ministers or civil servants. They may fear the executive, particularly for its capacity to do harm, but they do not respect it as they respect the judiciary. Judges, particularly of the higher courts, are by and large believed to be learned, high-minded, independent, dutiful and upright, qualities that one no longer associates with either ministers or their secretaries.

The high esteem enjoyed by the judiciary leads people to turn to it for remedies for the many ills suffered by society. There are two important indicators of the increasing reliance on the courts for addressing what may broadly be described as social problems. The first is the proliferation of public interest litigation, and the second is the tendency to formulate economic and social problems as matters of right rather than policy. How far and in what ways the judiciary will respond to this change in public attitudes will have major consequences for the operation of democracy in India.

Public interest litigation has caught the imagination of Indians with a social conscience. Its expansion has been accompanied by the growing importance of non-governmental organizations. It has increasingly exposed the weaknesses and defaults of the executive government and made citizens aware of the importance of their rights. Whereas universal elementary education was earlier treated as a matter of policy, it will become a matter of right through a proposed amendment to the constitution. The failure of policy is a failure of the executive whereas if something is made into a right it will acquire a greater measure of urgency; and where the administration failed to implement the policy, the courts may be trusted to see that the right is enforced.

It has not taken much time for our judges to see that the public has more trust in them than in the executive. Judges with an activist inclination will perhaps welcome a more central role in social engineering than was envisaged in the constitution. Responding to the misgivings expressed by some over the increase in judicial activism, Justice Ahmadi, then Chief Justice of India, had said in 1996 that 'the phenomenon of judicial activism in its aggressive role will have to be a temporary one'. In India what starts as a temporary phenomenon has an uncanny way of becoming permanent. If judicial activism leads to the further demoralization of the executive, it will not be a good thing for either the executive or the judiciary. In India the main work of governance has to be done by the executive, no matter how virtuous the judiciary is or how resourceful the non-governmental organizations are.

Are our judges more virtuous than our civil servants? Even if they are at the present time, one cannot count on their remaining so for all time and under all circumstances. Our judges and our civil servants come from the same social background, have had the same kind of education, and are shaped by broadly the same social forces. What applies to the civil service applies by and large to the judiciary as well: the higher judiciary is different in character and conduct from the lower, and the lower courts are not particularly notable as places of virtue.

The dignity, probity and rectitude that one associates with judges of the Supreme Court and of the high courts are due in no small measure to the greater autonomy they enjoy than their counterparts in the civil service. The business of governance requires civil servants to dirty their hands in ways in which judges do not have to dirty theirs; it is another matter that so many of the former become addicted to the dirt in which they deal. If judges do not pay the price that their autonomy demands, their character and conduct will come under the same public scrutiny to which the executive is subjected. And the judiciary has far fewer resources than the executive for defending itself in the face of public discontent.

49

The Administrative Executive

The administrative executive or the permanent civil service has an important part to play in the governance of the country. Yet it no longer enjoys a good standing with either the press or the public. It is accused of being at the same time insensitive to the needs of the common people and entangled with corrupt and unscrupulous politicians. Politicians publicly castigate civil servants for their obstructive and petty-minded ways while civil servants privately attribute all the failures of governance to the venality of their political masters. The working of constitutional democracy depends on a close collaboration between the political and the administrative executives, and endemic mistrust and hostility between them can hardly contribute to the success of governance. A good working relation between the two requires at the very least a clear perception of the differences of function between them.

In a constitutional democracy such as ours, the civil service operates through what may be called the bureaucratic mode of administration. The term 'bureaucracy' has today a negative connotation for citizens in all walks of life, and especially for intellectuals. There are two kinds of criticism made against the administrative executive in India: first, that it does not function as a proper bureaucracy; and second,

The Telegraph, 24 November 1997.

that it cannot be expected to serve the citizenry so long as it acts bureaucratically. It is the second view, that bureaucracy is inherently dysfunctional or that it is contrary to the spirit of democracy, that requires to be critically examined.

Bureaucratic administration operates through rational, impersonal rules. These rules are rational to the extent that they are man-made and subject to continuous review and revision with the conscious objective of making them consistent with each other and with the tasks set before the administration. The administration is impersonal in the sense that it is in principle based on the complete separation between what is official and what is private, requiring the official to act without fear or favour and without consideration of kin, caste and community. In a society where kin, caste and community loom so large, to disregard them altogether is to risk being accused of lacking in social sympathy.

If the enlightened citizen has everywhere a rather negative view of bureaucracy, this may be because he rarely thinks of any other system of administration to compare with it. If he were to choose between bureaucratic and patrimonial administration, he would almost certainly choose the former, if only as the lesser evil. Much of the public criticism of bureaucratic administration is misdirected. At least in this country, the failure of bureaucracy is most often its failure to insulate itself from contamination by patrimonialism. The conduct of administration by impersonal rules and the separation of the official from the private go against the grain of a society in which personal bonds predominate.

When the higher civil servant maintains distance from the everyday affairs of the local community, he is accused of being socially insensitive; when he takes too close an interest in them, he is suspected of being entangled in local politics. Many young and well-intentioned civil servants feel tempted to become social activists, but it is not easy for them to do so without compromising the obligations of their office.

Whereas the politician typically owes his position to election, the civil servant holds his office by appointment. In our case, this appointment is made on the basis of open, general competition where technical ability rather than social background is the criterion of selection. The Constitution of India guarantees equality of opportunity in matters of public employment for all citizens without consideration of caste, creed or community. But the abolition of legal impediments to equality of opportunity does not lead automatically to the removal of social obstacles. It is therefore natural to ask how far the equality of opportunity guaranteed in principle is in fact realized in practice.

Nowhere in the world does the higher civil service recruit its members equally from every section of society. It draws its recruits from the middle and the upper-middle classes in far greater proportions than the strength of those classes in the total population. Apart from providing them with better schooling, middle-class parents transmit substantial social and cultural advantages to their offspring that give them a clear edge in the competition for every kind of superior employment. This does not mean that individual ability and luck do not count at all, but they can outweigh social and cultural advantages to only a limited extent.

There has been some broadening of the social base of recruitment to the higher civil service in the last fifty years. This has come about through some expansion in education and of the middle classes in general. Since the removal of social as against purely legal impediments to upward social mobility takes time, only a few persons from disadvantaged strata can make their way into the higher civil service on their own if matters are left entirely to open competition.

But matters need not be left to open competition in recruitment to the higher civil service. The state can intervene directly in order to ensure that the major castes and communities are all represented in the administration in proportion to their strength in the population. Caste quotas have in fact been used since colonial times to give a more representative character to the bureaucracy. When first introduced into the bureaucracy by the British, they were attacked by the leaders of the nationalist movement as being divisive. They were not only retained after independence, but their scope has been greatly expanded. Caste quotas do not by themselves alter the middle-class character of the higher civil service, for a middle class has by now emerged among most castes and communities, and it is from this class that higher civil servants are still largely recruited.

Caste quotas cannot ensure that all classes and strata will be represented in the administrative executive in proportion to their strength in the population. No matter how artfully we devise a scheme of quotas, the higher civil service, if it is to function as an efficient bureaucracy, will continue to be recruited largely from the educated urban middle classes which still comprise a small part of the population of the country.

There is a more fundamental issue, namely, whether the administrative executive needs to be representative of the people to the same extent or in the same sense as the political executive. In a constitutional democracy, it is the elected political leader who performs a representational function; the appointed official performs an administrative and not a representational function. The civil servant is expected to serve all citizens without fear or favour, and without consideration of kin, caste and community. He does not have any particular constituency, and should not serve any particular interest. Civil servants recruited through public examinations are ill-equipped to perform representational functions, and can do so only ineptly and to the detriment of their allotted responsibilities. The confusion of roles between the elected leader and the appointed official will be to the advantage of neither, and will in the end undermine the basic values of constitutional democracy.

50

Recasting the Constitution

The government's proposal to review and possibly recast the Constitution of India has run into bad weather. This was to be expected in the present fractious political environment. The Congress party, now in opposition, could be counted on to find some reason to oppose what the BJP government wishes to do. The BJP's own allies have misgivings about how far the revision should go; and there are very strong differences of opinion within the Sangh Parivar itself about the basic structure of the constitution and what should be changed in it.

There are understandable, though perhaps exaggerated, fears about what may be done to the secular character of the Indian constitution on the pretext of bringing it in line with the Indian tradition. The opponents of secularism are artful; they will not attack it in the name of Hinduism or religion, but in that of tradition and morality. For all its limitations and shortcomings, the Indian constitution is forward and not backward looking. The values on which it rests—equality, liberty, rule of law, individual rights—are all modern and not traditional values. If those values have not been realized fully or even substantially in the last fifty years, this is not because of our present constitution, but in spite of it.

The Times of India, 4 May 2000.

Even the best of constitutions is not perfect: no man-made object can be. For those who agonize over secularism it is well to remember that there was not even the pretence of divinity in the making of the Indian constitution. What has been created by human beings can of course be amended and improved by other human beings. Indeed, it is in the nature of a modern constitution that it has built-in provisions for its own amendment. These provisions have been used somewhat freely in the fifty years since the constitution was adopted. Increasing numbers of persons have begun to feel that the time has come to go beyond these piecemeal changes and attempt something more comprehensive. But others feel that we have a good constitution and that the pro-changers should be restrained from making the best the enemy of the good.

The writing of a constitution or even its rewriting is a major event in the life of a nation. Certain conditions have to be met if the event is to be fruitful and effective. The first and most important of these is that there should be a consensus in the country about the desirable legal and political order and the desirable way for its creation and sustenance.

It will be hard to deny that the kind of consensus that existed between 15 August 1947 and 26 January 1950 does not exist today. It will not do to forget that a consensus did not exist when the Constituent Assembly had its first meetings in December 1946. The Muslim League boycotted the Assembly and the princely states went unrepresented. The consensus began to emerge only after partition and independence. Its creation, which is recorded in the official report of the debates conducted over three years in the Constituent Assembly, was a very impressive achievement. Should a constitution that was written when the consensus was strong be rewritten when it is weak?

As I have said, no human creation, whatever the conditions

of its creation, can be fully free from defect. If I were asked to point to one single defect in the Constitution of India, I would point to its excessive length. It is easily the lengthiest document of its kind. Its length is four times the combined lengths of the US and the French constitutions. It has too many provisions: and they are too specific, too detailed and too concrete. This has made the Constitution of India an unwieldy document. Paradoxically, it is its excessive length and detail that has forced so many amendments on it.

The historical tendency of Indian civilization has been one of accretion, leading to the accumulation of new elements without the elimination of old ones. It is very unlikely that a revision of the constitution will lead to a reduction of its length. If the committee set up for its review follows the general tendency, its length will almost certainly increase. The momentum of social and political change through legal and constitutional interventions has been towards the enlargement of constitutional provisions, and it is difficult to see a reversal of this momentum in the immediate future.

Some feel that the Indian constitution, unlike the older republican constitutions, such as the American or the French, has been used a little too freely with the object of changing the structure of society. In retrospect, the Constituent Assembly itself appears to have been a little too optimistic about what a brand new constitution could do to sweep away the age-old traditions, customs, prejudices, hierarchies, animosities and apathies rooted in the Indian soil. It is not clear whether the review committee will confine itself to recommendations relating to the structure of governance or feel encouraged to go deeper and propose changes, for instance, in the balance between Fundamental Rights and Directive Principles of State Policy.

There are many kindly and sympathetic persons in our

country who feel that the conditions of the deprived and the disadvantaged can be speedily improved by granting them more extensive rights. The constitution already has a battery of rights, but they feel that new ones, such as the right to education and the right to work, should be added. The problem with the Constitution of India is not that it has too few rights but that it has too many, and partly for that reason those rights are not always taken very seriously, even by the courts.

It would be wrong to pass judgement in advance on the work of any committee. At the same time, one cannot escape the thought that not all its members are likely to be free from the virus of competitive populism. That virus is no longer confined to legislators and party leaders but has made inroads into even the loftiest of public institutions. If the deliberations of the review committee lead to simplification and rationalization of the structure of governance, that will be all the good. But attempts to go beyond that in the name of social justice are not likely to bear fruit and may be counterproductive. Politicians may promise all things to all persons with impunity, but a constitution that carries a plethora of provisions that cannot be enforced does more harm than good to society.